Jesus Christ for Today's World

Dec 1998

Difficult Reading
Poor Translation

A few pearls of
wisdom...

Read pages #100 & 101

Oct 2000

Jürgen Moltmann

Jesus Christ
for Today's World

Translated by Margaret Kohl

FORTRESS PRESS
Minneapolis

JESUS CHRIST FOR TODAY'S WORLD

First Fortress Press edition published 1994.

Translated by Margaret Kohl from the German, *Wer ist Christus für uns heute?* published by Gütersloh Kaiser, Germany, 1994. English translation copyright © 1994 Margaret Kohl. All rights reserved.

Cover painting: *Pietà* by Bernard Buffet (The National Museum of Modern Art, Paris).

Library of Congress Cataloging-in-Publication data
Moltmann, Jürgen.
    [Wer ist Christus für uns heute? English]
    Jesus Christ for today's world / Jürgen Moltmann; translated by Margaret Kohl.
        p. cm.
    Includes bibliographical references (p. 148–150) and index.
    ISBN 0–8006–2817–9:
    1. Jesus Christ — Person and offices.   I. Title.
BT202.M552413   1994
    232—dc20   94–13407
                                                                    CIP

Manufactured in Great Britain   1–2817

98   97   96   3   4   5   6   7   8   9   10

Contents

Who is Christ for Us Today?

The assurance of Christian faith depends on the answer to this question, and today the answers are multifarious and have become deeply uncertain. There is Western pluralism, in which faith turns into a private and optional affair. There is secularism, in which for many people faith becomes superfluous and a matter of indifference. But above all there is Christianity's own history, which for Jews and other peoples, and for the earth and other living things, has been and still is a history of suffering. Where is God, when people suffer under the violence of other human beings? Where is the kingdom of God, with peace and justice for everyone? Is there any future for humanity after Hiroshima? Is there any future for this earth after Chernobyl? We have become unsure, and are searching for someone or something that can give us hope for ourselves and our world. We are searching for 'the Christ'. Faced with our hopelessness today, we turn back to yesterday's answers, examining them and trying to translate them into our own time; and where they fall short, we try out new answers – our own answers. We live with these answers, and discover how far they take us, and where they too come up against a dead end.

Who is Christ for us today? The answer to this question is

not just an intellectual one. It is always life's own answer too. Acknowledgment of Christ and discipleship of Christ are two sides of the same thing: life in companionship with Christ. We need an answer to our questions which we can live and die with. That means that every christology is related to christopraxis: what we know and what we do belong together. And practice is the touchstone against which a christology's authenticity has to be tested. We believe in Christ with all our senses and with the lives we live, just as believing in God too can only mean believing with all our hearts and all our senses.

Who is Christ for me? I don't want to evade this personal question through generalities, so I will begin with a personal memory. In 1945 I was imprisoned in a wretched prisoner-of-war camp in Belgium. The German Reich had collapsed. German civilization had been destroyed through Auschwitz. My home town Hamburg lay in ruins; and in my own self things looked no different. I felt abandoned by God and human beings, and the hopes of my youth died. I couldn't see any future ahead of me. In this situation an American chaplain put a Bible into my hands, and I began to read it. First of all the psalms of lament in the Old Testament: 'I have fallen dumb and have to eat up my suffering within myself' (Luther's forceful translation) '. . . I am a stranger as all my fathers were' (Psalm 39). Then I was drawn to the story of the passion, and when I came to Jesus' death cry I knew: this is the one who understands you and is beside you when everyone else abandons you. 'My God, why have you forsaken me?' That was my cry for God too. I began to understand the suffering, assailed and God-forsaken Jesus, because I felt that he understood me. And I grasped that this Jesus is the divine Brother in our distress. He brings hope to the prisoners and the abandoned. He is the one who delivers us from the guilt that weighs us down and robs us of every

2

kind of future. And I became possessed by a hope when in human terms there was little enough to hope for. I summoned up the courage to live, at a point when one would perhaps willingly have put an end to it all. This early companionship with Jesus, the brother in suffering and the liberator from guilt, has never left me since. The Christ for me is the crucified Jesus.

In the public and private conflicts of my life I then also came to understand the presence of the earthly Jesus too: the one who brings God's kingdom to the poor, heals the sick, accepts the despised, calls people to discipleship and draws and wins us for a life with his hope and his tasks. It was above all the early protests against 'nuclear death' which convinced me of this, and then, later, the peace movement. It was only relatively late on that I perceived that this earthly Jesus – the Jesus of discipleship and God's kingdom – is the Jewish Jesus. Christian-Jewish dialogue opened my eyes to this. But at the same time it showed me my own Christian identity, which has its foundation in Jesus' new experience of God: 'Today this scripture has been fulfilled in your hearing' (Luke 4.21). This divine Today means that Jesus' earthly life is messianic through and through, lit up by Israel's hope and radiating hope for the peace of the world: Israel's messiah, the saviour of the nations. I have always missed this presence of the earthly Jesus in the Christian creeds. Why is it reduced to a mere comma between 'born' and 'suffered'? Ought we not to add – at least in thought –

Baptized by John the Baptist,
filled with the Holy Spirit
to proclaim God's kingdom to the poor,
to heal the sick,
to receive the rejected,

to awaken Israel for the salvation of the nations,
and to have mercy on all human beings?

But as well as this early recognition of Jesus as the brother who suffers with us, the Easter faith came to be important for me too. Of course the symbols of raising and resurrection are drawn from an earlier era, when people talked in mythical pictures and images about God's marvellous intervention in this world. But it is only their outward form which is tied to this world picture. In our own experience, faith in the resurrection is confronted by the death to which we are surrendered. For me, faith in the resurrection is the faith in God of lovers and the dying, the suffering and the mourners. So it is no myth. The resurrection faith acquires its meaning in the struggles of love against death. We already experience resurrection here and now, in the midst of life, when we rise up against death in life, against the oppressions and the hurts to which life here is subjected. In love, resurrection is not merely expected; it is already experienced. For love makes us come alive. And love never gives anyone or anything up for lost. It sees a future in which God will restore everything, and put everything to rights, and gather everything into his kingdom. This great hope strengthens our little hopes, and puts them straight. It is the presence of Jesus in the Spirit of life.

The chapters of this book have grown out of lectures which I have given in Germany and many other countries, and which I have discussed with a wide variety of people and groups. These discussions suggested the method of looking at the material in three chapters or stages: first seeing what the biblical writings have to say; then moving towards a theological judgment by way of questions and answers; and finally enquiring about guidelines for action. We shall be searching for approaches which will help us to answer the question: who is Christ for us today? I am not proposing to

4

offer a complete christology here; for that I may point to my book *The Way of Jesus Christ: Christology in Messianic Dimensions* (1989; English edition 1990).

I should like to thank Thomas Kucharz and Steffen Lösel for their work on the present texts.

Tübingen, 9 May 1993   Jürgen Moltmann

I

Jesus and the Kingdom of God

1. The kingdom of God and Jesus

Anyone who gets involved with Jesus gets involved with the kingdom of God. This is an inescapable fact, for Jesus' own concern was, and is, God's kingdom. Anyone who looks for God and asks about the kingdom in which 'righteousness and peace kiss one another' (Ps. 85.10) should look at Jesus and enter into the things that happened in his presence and that still happen today in his Spirit. That is obviously and palpably true; for who is Jesus? Simply *the kingdom of God in person*.

The two belong inseparably together: Jesus and the kingdom of God – the kingdom of God and Jesus. Jesus brings God's kingdom to us human beings in his own unique way, and guides us into the breadth and beauty of the kingdom. And God's kingdom makes Jesus the Christ, the saviour and deliverer for us all. So if we want to learn what that mysterious 'kingdom of God' really is, we have to look at Jesus. And if we want to understand who Jesus really is, we have to experience the kingdom of God.

2. 'The kingdom of God': biblical perspectives

Trouble already begins with the translation, if terms are used which make the reader think of something different from what the text means to say. *Basileia tou Theou* says the Greek. How ought we to translate that? 'Kingdom,' says English; 'Reich' – empire – says German. If we say 'the kingdom of God', some people will think of the United Kingdom; others will think of the Roman empire, or the German Reich – at all events a kingdom or empire of some kind, even if a 'holy' one. A kingdom or empire is certainly an area with a shared law and a common government, and inhabited by its own citizens. If what we mean is a particular space or sector, we talk about 'the realm of the good' and 'the realm of evil', and about 'the two kingdoms', the one spiritual and the other secular. But if the kingdom has to do with God, there cannot be two or more kingdoms, because God is one and there is no one besides him.

For the last hundred years or so, the translation 'rule of God' has come to be frequently used instead of 'kingdom of God'. That sounds more dynamic: God is the Lord because he rules, and everything he rules over is his kingdom. So far so good – but not really so good at all, for we have suffered under so many kinds of seizures of power in personal, professional and political life that we have become cautious about yearning for a 'divine rule'. We should like to know first *how* God rules – how his rule compares with all these other forms of domination, and whether all of us – his obedient servants and 'handmaids' – have any say in it too.

For God simply to be 'the Lord' may perhaps please men well enough; but women who have become sensitive to the matter find that to expect them to assent to this attribute is a tall order; they have, understandably enough, little or no desire for any more 'lordship'. But more and more men are rejecting the notion of being 'lords' or 'masters' too. They want to be accepted as brothers and friends.

If the phrase 'rule of God' is heightened even more through the translation 'royal rule of God', then even in confirmation classes one has to look far and wide for a useful comparison without straying into the columns of the tabloids, with their gossip about kings and princesses.

If we open the New Testament, we find that it doesn't give a definition of the kingdom of God at all. Jesus never explicitly explained 'the concept' of the kingdom. 'Jesus assumes that what the term means is familiar', says a recent church memorandum in Germany. So one might perhaps think; but it is not in fact true. Jesus provided us with no old or new 'concept' of the kingdom of God at all. He brought God's kingdom himself. That is something very different. It is one thing to define the proper concepts about life, and quite another to live rightly. It is one thing to learn a concept of happiness, and another to be happy. And so it is one thing to reduce the kingdom of God to a definition, and another to experience it, to feel it, to see it and to taste it. It is not the term which must be allowed to define the experience. The experience must define the term. Otherwise we could be prevented by a plethora of sheer concepts from having any new experiences at all.

So let us leave the concepts for 'Jesus' concern' where they are and turn to the thing itself. How was Jesus describing his 'concern' when he could say 'it is in the midst of us'? How were people experiencing 'his concern' when they exulted: 'That which we have heard, which we have seen with our eyes, which we have looked upon and touched with our hands: the word of life' (I John 1.1)?

Following the method 'see – judge – act', we shall begin with four biblical perspectives. Then we shall go on to discuss five theological questions and answers; and finally we shall explore the practical consequences which follow on the experience and expectation of God's kingdom.

The special thing about Jesus is that he talks about the kingdom of God in *comparisons*, or parables, which he takes from the world of nature and the world of human beings. These bring the kingdom of God close to us in a way no definition could do. We enter into Jesus' healings because these miracles are miracles of God's kingdom. We look at Jesus' shared meals with marginalized men and women – 'tax collectors and sinners' – because they mean eating and drinking in God's kingdom. Finally we hear the 'basic law' of God's kingdom – its constitution, so to speak – in the Beatitudes in the Sermon on the Mount.

First perspective: the kingdom of God in the parables

In Mark's Gospel chapter 4 we find a group of parables drawn from the dealings of human beings with nature: the parables of the sower and the seed, and the parable of the mustard seed. These are pictures or images of beginnings, life-processes of hope. The person who 'goes out to sow' scatters the seed on the earth because he hopes that it will grow and bring fruit. This is like the kingdom of God: the seed is sown in our lives so that it may grow and bring fruit in us. The beginnings are small, but if these beginnings are God's, the effects will be great and marvellous. The seeds of the kingdom are like mustard seed, 'the smallest of all the seeds'. But when they germinate they grow into trees big enough for the birds to nest in. The seed grows automatically, all by itself, day and night. Its inner strength develops into blade, and ear, and the field of wheat. If we don't just concentrate on the transferred sense but look at the original one too, we can see the kingdom of God as the reawakening of nature. That is why Mark 13.28f. compares God's kingdom with summer time.

Nature itself becomes the parable. In spring the trees become green, the flowers bud, and the seed springs up in the fields; and in the same way the kingdom of God is the final springtime of creation. New life begins; everything that has been created comes alive and becomes fruitful. We notice that the parables are taken from spring and summer, not from autumn and winter. Nature's cycle is growth and decay, becoming and dying. But it is only the becoming that is adopted as a parable for God's kingdom. Why? Because the kingdom of God is nothing other than the new creation of all things for eternal life.

The nature parables make the kingdom of God something quite sensory: I smell a rose, and with it smell the kingdom of God. I taste bread and wine, and taste the kingdom of God. I walk through a meadow bright with flowers, and feel the kingdom where everything can grow and unfold: the kingdom in which there is enough for everyone.

In Luke chapter 15 we have another group of parables – the lost and found parables: the lost sheep, the lost coin, the lost son. There is joy in heaven over one 'sinner who repents' (15.7) more than over ninety-nine just and righteous people; just as the shepherd who has left his ninety-nine sheep to their own devices delights at finding the one he has lost. We are pleased to find that the second parable is about a woman, the woman who loses her silver coin and finds it again. Again we are told 'there is joy before the angels of God over one sinner who repents'. And then follows the parable about the lost son – the 'prodigal' son, as we know him. Here the father's joy is so great that he says: 'This my son was dead, and is alive again; he was lost, and is found' (15.24). In the summings-up of Jesus' message we are also told again and again: 'The kingdom of God is at hand – repent.' But what does the word 'repent' really mean according to these parables?

A sheep has gone astray and is found, and *the finder* is delighted that his search has not been in vain. The lost coin could do nothing about either its loss or its finding; the joy is solely and entirely the woman's. The lost son, finally, was not merely 'lost and found'; he had actually been 'dead and was alive again'. So if we look at these parables, what is the kingdom of God? It is nothing other than God's joy at finding again the beings he created who have been lost. And what is the 'repentance' which the sinner has to 'perform'? It is nothing other than the being-found, and the return home from exile and estrangement, the coming-alive again, and the joining in God's joy. We are experiencing God's kingdom when something like this happens to us, something where we flower and put out fresh growth like the flowers and trees in the spring, and come alive again, because we sense the great, inexhaustible love from which all life proceeds. When we experience God's exhilaration in his joy over us, and our own vitality reawakens, the kingdom of God ceases to be some remote and alien rule; it is the very source and fountain of life. Then the kingdom of God is *the wide space* in which we can unfold and develop, because it is a place without any restrictions. Once we experience God's kingdom like this, we discover afresh the wealth of our potentialities for living.

Second perspective: the kingdom of God in the healing of the sick

The first thing that people discovered about Jesus, the Gospels tell us, was the healing power of the divine Spirit. So in the Gospels, the people surrounding Jesus are not shown as 'sinners' (as they are in Paul) but as people who are sick. They creep forward out of the corners and shadows into which they have been pushed, and try to get close to Jesus. 'That evening, at sundown, they brought to him all who were sick or

12

possessed with demons. And the whole city was gathered together about the door. And he healed many who were sick with various diseases, and cast out many demons' (Mark 1.32ff.). Demons are forces of derangement and destruction, thought of in personal terms. They are characterized by their delight in tormenting. When the Messiah comes, says the old Jewish hope, these tormenting spirits will disappear from the earth, and people will be restored to health and reason. Miraculous healings were common enough in the ancient world. We find them in our modern world of scientific medicine too. But with Jesus they have a special context. They are part of the coming of God's kingdom. When the living God comes to his creation, the powers of torment are forced to retreat, and the created beings they have tortured will be made well again. The kingdom of the living God drives out the germs of death and spreads the seeds of life. It doesn't merely bring salvation in a religious sense. It brings health in bodily experience too. In the healing of the sick the kingdom takes bodily form. The Spirit makes what is sick and dying alive again. Today, many of us have no personal access to these stories about Jesus' healings, because we have never experienced anything comparable; but even so, these stories help us to understand that the divine vitality desires to penetrate our bodies too; and we shall comprehend the organic side of the kingdom of God.

When God comes and renews the disrupted and deranged world, it is not extraordinary that the sick should be healed and the germs of illness disappear. It is a matter of course. Jesus' healings are 'miracles of the kingdom'. In the daybreak radiance of the new creation of all things, they are not miracles at all; they are entirely a matter of course. Certainly, if we lose the great hope of the kingdom of God and can no longer look ahead, these stories of healings turn into fairytales which can be forgotten. But in the framework of hope for God's kingdom they cannot be forgotten, for in that framework they become reminders of hope.

All severe illnesses are heralds or foretokens of death, and we have to see Jesus' healings as heralds or foretokens in just the same way: they are heralds of the resurrection. It is only when this mortal life is reborn to eternal life that what Jesus did for the dead will be completed. In every serious illness we fight for our lives. In every healing we experience something of the resurrection. We feel new-born, and as if life had been given back to us. That is how it will be when that happens which we cannot begin to imagine, because we have never yet experienced it: the resurrection of the dead and the life of the world to come.

In that resurrection world the kingdom of God will be completed, the kingdom whose seeds Jesus has planted in our hearts through his words, and in our bodies through his healings. When we think of sickness, God's kingdom means healing; when we think of death it means resurrection.

Jesus made God's kingdom his own concern by healing the sick. That is true, but it is only half the truth. For because men and women who were sick came to him, Jesus himself experienced what the kingdom of God is too. He did not have the divine power of healing at his own disposal. In certain relationships there were healings – in others nothing happened at all. In his home town Nazareth 'he could not do a single mighty work', we are told in Mark 6.5. What were the conditions under which Jesus' healing power could act?

When a sick boy is brought to him, Jesus implores the father: 'If you could only believe! All things are possible for the person who believes.' The boy's father answers through his tears: 'I do believe, Lord – help my unbelief' (Mark 9.23–24). That little bit of unbelieving belief is enough. Jesus 'took the boy by the hand and lifted him up and he arose'. The stories about sick women speak a more powerful language still. There is the woman 'with an issue of blood' (Mark 5.25ff.). She creeps through the crowd from behind until she has reached Jesus and takes hold of his coat. 'If I could only just touch his clothes I should be well again', she says to herself. By touching Jesus she makes him 'unclean', as people thought then. But she extorts her own healing from him. Jesus 'perceived in himself that power had gone forth from him'. He looks at her and says: 'My daughter, your faith has made you well; go in peace.' He experiences the healing power which goes out from him without his will, and learns to know this healing power through the faith of the sick woman. He grows from the expectations of the sick and in this atmosphere learns what the kingdom of God in its reality is.

The kingdom of God, we might say, is what happens between Jesus and the sick, between his power and the faith of men and women. The two things have to come together. When they do, we talk about an experience of the Holy Spirit. The presence of God's kingdom is discovered in experiences of the Spirit like this. The future of this experience of the Spirit is that kingdom. So today too we experience the coming kingdom in the present Spirit of God who brings us to life and makes us living people.

Third perspective: the kingdom of God in the companionship of Jesus

Jesus promised God's kingdom to the poor, and bestowed God's power on the sick; and in the same way he brought God's justice to people who knew no justice and to the unjust – to the people the Bible calls 'sinners and tax collectors'. He demonstrated this publicly through his companionship with them. 'This man receives sinners and eats with them', say the respectable people, annoyed (Luke 15.2). But against the horizon of God's imminent kingdom, by sitting down at table

15

with unjust people Jesus was anticipating the eating and drinking of the just and righteous in the kingdom of God.

'The banquet of the righteous' shared with these unjust and unrighteous people? Yes, for through his compassion with them he practised the divine justice of grace, and 'justified' them, as Paul was later to put it – he 'made them just'. This is already implicit in the word 'received'. The self-respect of anyone who is shut out and rejected is profoundly injured. We feel 'like dirt'. And if we accept this judgment and make it our own, we begin to despise and hate ourselves. But if in a situation of this kind we find people who accept and affirm us without any reservations, because they have hope for us, we feel strengthened and as if liberated. The acceptance of despised people is the social healing which Jesus brings 'sinners and tax collectors'. In this way the kingdom of God comes into the world of the humiliated and insulted, and breaks open the psychological prisons of self-contempt.

But wherever there are people who have been pushed out, like these 'sinners and tax collectors', they are balanced on the other side by the people who are just and good; these are the ones who decide what is just and what is unjust, and who is good and who is bad. The possession of wealth makes the have-nots poor, and the possession of the good makes the bad people bad. When Jesus 'receives sinners and eats with them', for the good people he is either a sinner himself, or a revolutionary who is disrupting society's system of values. But by 'justifying' sinners he saves the good and the just too, because he liberates them from their self-righteousness. The person who accepts sinners is prepared to accept the just as well – but not as the just: as sinners. It is the very same justice of grace which saves the one and judges the other so that they may all arrive at peace together.

Fourth perspective: the kingdom of the poor and the children

The constitution or 'basic law' of the kingdom of God in this world is Jesus' Sermon on the Mount, and that reaches its climax in the Beatitudes, which call the poor 'blessed' because 'the kingdom of heaven is theirs'. What Paul and the people of the Reformation called 'the justification of sinners' is in Jesus the calling of the poor blessed. The gospel is preached to 'the poor': first of all to the people who in the world *are* nothing and *have* nothing. The collective term 'the poor' embraces the hungry, the unemployed, the enslaved, the people who have lost heart and lost hope, and the suffering. It means the oppressed people itself as a whole – the people Greek calls *ochlos* and Korean *minjung*. The poor are socially the non-persons, the work force, human fodder; and as a rule the poorest of the poor were, and still are, old women who are allegedly 'no more use'.

At the other end of society are not merely 'the rich'. There are also the violent, who make the poor poor, enriching themselves at their expense or simply pushing the weaker people out. Again, with what he says and does Jesus enters into the social conflicts of a violent society which makes the rich richer and the poor poorer. Again, the gospel about God's kingdom takes sides in this conflict. It takes sides with the poor in order to save the rich and to liberate them from their self-complacency.

What does the gospel bring the poor? Not charitable works. Nor does it make them just as rich as the rest. What it does do is to give them new dignity and a powerful stimulus. The poor are no longer the suffering objects of oppression and humiliation. They are their own determining subjects, with the dignity of God's first children. Jesus brings the poor the certainty of their indestructible dignity in God's eyes. And with this awareness, people who are poor, slaves, and women who have been sold

17

can get up out of the dust and help themselves. They throw aside the values of the society which daily dins into their ears: 'You're failures! You haven't made it! You're good for nothing!' They begin to live with their heads held high, and an upright walk. An inner acceptance of the meritocracy's system of values is always the greatest hindrance to the self-liberation of the poor, because this acceptance engenders self-contempt. Faith overcomes this self-hate and raises up those who are bowed down. 'The kingdom of heaven is yours' is not cheap consolation, a sop designed to keep the poor quiet. It is the authority to get up and bring peace to this world of violence, as children of God's kingdom. Jesus doesn't set the poor on the road to social advancement, so that they can be as rich as the rest. He sets them on the road of fellowship, whose culture is the culture of sharing, as the feeding of the five thousand shows.

Jesus and his men and women disciples proclaimed to the poor of their time their future in the kingdom of God, because the kingdom already belongs to the poor. 'Blessed are the poor, for theirs is the kingdom of heaven' (Matt. 5.3). Jesus discovers God's kingdom among the poor. The poor show him God's kingdom. The same happens with the children. He says that the kingdom of heaven already 'belongs' to them (Matt. 19.14), discovering from them that people have to become 'like children' if they want to enter God's kingdom. So there really is a silent invitation to the kingdom of God which comes from the poor – whether we like to call it 'evangelization through the poor' or 'the messianism of the poor' is not important. And there is also a very simple and unspoken invitation to the kingdom of God through children.

Anyone of us who hears about the kingdom in Jesus' message discovers the same kingdom in his companionship with the poor and with women and children. These 'last' are the first with God, and these weakest of the weak are the strongest. It is good to know whom we can have recourse to. The one who brought the kingdom of God close to us brings the poor and the children close to us too. They are his family, his people, for they too represent God's kingdom in this world of violence.

3. Some theological clarifications

Taking these biblical insights as our basis, let us now try to answer some theological questions which come up again and again when we talk about 'the kingdom of God'.

First question: Is the kingdom of God present or future?

Is it something we already experience or something we expect and wait for? After what we have already said, the answer is not difficult. *God's kingdom is experienced in the present* in companionship with Jesus. Where the sick are healed and the lost are found, where people who are despised are accepted and the poor discover their own dignity, where people who have become rigid and fossilized come alive again, and old, tired life becomes young and fruitful once more – there the kingdom of God begins. It begins as a seed. The germs of it are already implanted in this life, so it can be experienced. Being a seed, it is also *the object of hope*, but a hope firmly founded on experience and remembrance: the seed wants to grow, the one who has been found wants to return home, those who have been healed want to rise from the dead, and people liberated from some compulsion want to live in the country of freedom. Just because in the companionship of Jesus the kingdom of God is experienced in the present, its completion is hoped for in the future. Experience and hope strengthen one another mutually.

Second question: Does the kingdom of God belong to this world, like an earthly kingdom, or is it a heavenly kingdom in the next?

The people who would like to see it as belonging to the next world always point to Jesus' saying that 'my kingdom is not of this world' (John 18.36). But in so doing they are overlooking the fact that this is a statement about the origin of the kingdom, not its place. Of course it is not 'of' this world, in the sense of coming from it. It comes from God. If it didn't come from God, it couldn't heal this sick world. But in and through Jesus it is in the midst of this world, and when Jesus said these words the kingdom of God in person was standing in front of Rome's imperial governor, Pontius Pilate. If it is the kingdom of the creator God, then it embraces the whole of creation, heaven and earth, the invisible side of the world and the visible side too; so it is both in the next world, in heaven, and in this one, on earth. In the Lord's Prayer, we pray for the coming of the kingdom 'on earth as it is in heaven', meaning by heaven the side of creation which already corresponds wholly to God, and by earth the side of creation which is still in dispute. We expect from the future of the kingdom a new heaven *and* a new earth. So there is no salvation without this earth. God's kingdom is as earthly as Jesus himself was, and anyone who looks at Jesus' end will say: through the cross of Christ the kingdom of God is ineradicably implanted on this earth. With the resurrection of the crucified Christ the rebirth of the whole tormented creation begins. So 'remain true to the earth'! For the earth is worth it.

Third question: Is the kingdom of God simply God's own affair, or is it something in which men and women are involved too? Can we do nothing about it or can we perform messianic works as well?

'God's kingdom is God's business', ecclesiastical declarations like to say, in order to come to the conclusion: 'Men and women cannot set up this kingdom and are not required to do so' (Magdeburg Declaration of October 1988). This amicable separation between God and human beings is understandable in the light of the Western world's modern alternative – the alternative between God and human freedom. But it puts an end to everything that the New Testament says about Jesus. Where is Jesus in this partition? Was he God? Was he a human being? Was he not the divine human being, God-become-human? That at least is what all the Christian creeds say he was. So the first part of the sentence is wrong. It must read: *God's kingdom is Jesus' affair.*

As we have seen, in community with Jesus men and women experienced God's kingdom with their senses and in their bodies, not just provisionally and ambivalently, but as unequivocally as a sick person is restored to health, a sinner is accepted, and someone who has been lost is found. As Jesus' affair, the kingdom of God is experienced in real, practical terms. And equally, it can be practised in just these real, practical terms by men and women. 'Seek first the kingdom of God and his righteousness . . .'

In the companionship of Jesus the power of God is experienced. Through this experience people become 'co-workers for the kingdom of God' and do the same messianic work as Jesus himself: 'Go and preach: the kingdom of God is at hand. Heal the sick, raise the dead, cleanse lepers, cast out demons' (Matt. 10.7–8). So according to what Jesus intended *the kingdom of God is our affair too.*

In nineteenth-century Germany, 'kingdom-of-God work'

21

was the description quite rightly given to missionary and diaconic ministries carried out by Christians in the world. Kingdom-of-God work – that was Johann Hinrich Wichern's 'Rauhe Haus' for neglected children in Hamburg; that is what the industrial concerns were which Gustav Werner organized on co-operative lines in Reutlingen; that was Bodelschwingh's idea of diaconic institutions for the handicapped in Bethel. I could give as examples Kagawa's 'kingdom of God movement' in the Tokyo slums, the base communities in Latin America, and the peace movement in Germany. Everywhere God's kingdom takes us beyond the frontiers of the church.

But when we are thinking about the Protestant work ethic of modern times, there is something important to be added as well. Just because of this kingdom-of-God work, and therefore parallel to it, there is *delight* in the kingdom of God too, delight which finds expression in sabbath rest and the celebration of God's feast. According to the Jewish view, a sabbath rightly celebrated is 'a sixtieth' of the kingdom of God, and every feast of God's in its true fruition is more than that. It is good to 'work and pray', but rest and celebration belong to the completion too.

Fourth question: Is the kingdom of God a different world, or does it mean that this world will be different?

Some people imagine that the kingdom of God will be a different world, which will come about when this one ends. Some people imagine that eternal life will be a different life, a life after death, which will follow when this life is finished. But this puts us on the wrong track and leads us to undervalue God's creation.

The new creation is not a different creation. It is the new creation of this deranged world. Eternal life is not a different life. It is the resurrection of this life into the life of God. 'This

22

perishable nature must put on the imperishable, and this mortal nature must put on immortality', Paul stresses (I Cor. 15.53). So the kingdom of God means that this world will be different and will be born anew out of violence and injustice to justice, righteousness and peace. Consequently God's kingdom cannot be restricted to any religious, moral or spiritual sphere. As the kingdom of the Creator God, it is as universal, protean and multifarious as this whole rich creation. Even if as yet we only experience the seed and the germ, the waking up in the morning and restoration to health after we have been ill, we have no right to set limits to the new creation of all things, or to keep the kingdom of God out of the market economy or world politics. Wherever life is threatened, the living God gets involved, for he loves life.

Fifth question: Is the kingdom of God a theocracy, or is it union with the living God?

If the phrase 'the kingdom of God' is translated as 'the rule of God', there is an overtone of theocracy about it; but 'Jesus' concern' stresses the coming to fresh life of all created beings in the community of the Creator. The kingdom of God is 'the wide space in which there is no more cramping'. There is no human liberty without this free space of God's. The kingdom of God: that is full-filled time, the moment when it is truly permissible to say with Goethe's Faust: 'O tarry a while, thou art so fair', because it does indeed 'tarry' or remain, and is without end. The kingdom of God: that is God when he has arrived at his rest, God dwelling in his creation, and making it his house, his home. All created beings will share this home with him. The kingdom of God: that means that God is close and wholly present, and lets those he has created participate in his attributes, the things that characterize him – his glory and his beauty, his livingness and his goodness; for God also participates in the attributes of those he has created – in their finitude, their vulnerability and their mortality. The kingdom of God: we already experience it here in love, for 'he who abides in love abides in God, and God in him' (I John 4.16). So we expect it there too: the redeemed creation in God, and the rejoicing God in creation. I may call this interpretation the Christian view of the kingdom of God. If Christ is God's kingdom in person, what else is God's kingdom but the cosmic incarnation of God? Without this Christian interpretation of the kingdom of God which we find with Jesus, the theocratic interpretation has no content and is exposed to clerical or political misuse.

4. 'First the kingdom of God . . .'

'Seek first the kingdom of God and his righteousness, and all these things shall be yours as well' (Matt. 6.33). For Jesus, the kingdom of God was always at the head of the agenda. With us, other things continually get in the way – usually our own interests. But what does it mean, to put the kingdom of God first in our lives again?

Let me take up the old idea about the different forms of the kingdom of God in this world, but divest them of their static character of unchangeable order. Instead let me suggest in more practical terms what we ought to aim at in these various sectors of life, in the interests of the kingdom of God. It is a matter of

1. humanizing conditions and relationships between people,
2. democratizing politics,
3. socializing the economy,

4. naturalizing civilization, and
5. making the kingdom of God the church's lodestone.

1. Marriage, family, friendships and relationships are the most intimate sectors in which men and women can become truly human. Because every act of inhumanity between husband and wife, parents and children, friend and friend is directly hurtful, the task facing us is to become truly human people and Christians in our dealings with one another and for one another.

The art of loving has to be learnt. We learn it through joy in each other, through the forgiveness of guilt we experience, and through the continually astonishing miracle of the new beginning. In that 'wide space where there is no cramping' we accept one another, grow with one another and unfold from one another. Part of love is friendship, which knows how to combine affection with respect for the other person's liberty. That means respect for the mystery of the other, and his or her still latent and unrealized potentialities. If love stops, we make a fixed image of each other. We judge and pin each other down. That is death. But love liberates us from these images and keeps the future open for the other person. We have hope for each other, so we wait for one another. That is life. Human relationships are more than marriage and the family. They are the foundation of every society. This means that in the name of 'Jesus' concern' a society is as good as the fortunes of its weakest members. The justice of compassion does not merely apply in charitable work and diaconic service. It has its place in the very constitution of every society which claims to be humane. Social legislation and an organized health service have to be judged by the burdens of the poor and the alleviation of the sick. Anyone who wants to know just how humane a society is must go into its prisons too. With the eyes of the crucified Christ, one sees society from below, as it were.

2. The democratization of politics is the programme which makes human and civil rights the point of departure, and organizes state institutions in such a way that they are there for people, not people for the state. Today governmental power and the exercise of power anywhere in the world can be legitimated only under the overriding criterion of human dignity and human rights. This is true not only for a country's internal policies; it applies to its foreign policy too. State power and the exercise of power are limited by human rights; if these limits are crossed, they lose their legitimacy. That is why Thesis 5 of the Barmen Theological Declaration says: 'The church is a reminder of God's kingdom, God's command-ments and righteousness, and hence of the responsibility of governments and the governed.' In my view, remembrance of the kingdom of God forbids governments and the governed to 'deter' their potential enemies by threatening to destroy the world through ABC weapons. But remembrance of the kingdom of God also enjoins us, in my view, to intervene in the internal affairs of other countries if human rights are trampled under foot there.

3. Socializing the economy does not mean expropriation and nationalization. It means the just distribution of opportunities for work and profits – a distribution that is just towards everyone concerned, which means men *and* women, as well as people belonging to both the present generation *and* generations to come. Every society has a social contract which it has worked out for itself. But there is a contract between the generations too, and this has not been worked out. Today, as I believe, we have to ensure that there is (*a*) a just distribution of opportunities for work and for living, right across society, in a horizontal section; and (*b*) a just distribution of opportunities for work and for living in the longitudinal section of present and coming generations. Because children are the weakest members, and because coming generations have no say in

26

today's decisions, the costs of present profits are shuffled off on to them. This contravenes the justice of the kingdom of God.

4. Naturalizing our civilization means the ecological reform which is so urgently needed today. Up to now the aim of civilization has been to subjugate nature and make it of utility for human beings. A future civilization will have to integrate itself in the cosmic conditions which are the framework of the earth, and will have to observe the rights of fellow creatures and created things too, if humanity is to survive. The natural world in which we share must be protected against the rapacious and destructive grasp of human beings, for their own sake. It sounds like a paradox but it is simply true to say that it is only if human beings cease to be the centre of their civilization that humanity has a chance to survive. Human beings are not the crown of creation, nor was everything created for their sakes. Human beings are created beings in the great community of creation, made for the praise of God, like the heavens too, which 'declare his glory'.

5. The church must once again become an extroverted church which takes its bearing from the kingdom of God; it must renounce its modern, introverted orientation which tries to make the kingdom of God take its bearings from the church. The church is not there for its own sake. It is there for the sake of 'Jesus' concern'. All the church's own interests – its continuation in its existing form, the extension of its influence – must be subordinated to the interests of the kingdom of God. Otherwise they are unjustifiable. If the spirit and institutions of the church are in line with God's kingdom, then the church is Christ's church. If they run counter to God's kingdom, the church loses its right to exist and becomes a superfluous religious society. Today, for the church to make the kingdom of God its lodestone means *evangelization and liberation*. The church's divine mission is to proclaim the gospel of God's

27

kingdom to all human beings, the poor of this world first of all, so as to awaken the faith which consoles and strengthens us here and gives the certainty of eternal life. And at the same time the church's divine mission is to bring liberty to the oppressed, human dignity to the humiliated, and the justice which is their due to people without rights. Evangelization and liberation complement one another, like the raising up through faith of the soul that is bowed down and the healing of the tormented body. That is the message of the base communities and congregations among the people of Latin America, Asia and Africa – that these two things belong indissolubly together: Christ's missionary charge and the revolutionary imperative; the preaching of repentance and the transformation of unjust economic and political conditions into better justice; peace with God and the struggle for a peaceful world. Where the kingdom of God is near, God's people gather together. Then they proclaim the message of the kingdom and lead the world to the conversion that will save it. The church is an evangelizing and a liberating community. If it is not, it is not Christ's church – nor indeed a church at all.

To put it in a nutshell, these consequences mean:

First the kingdom of God and then the church:

We can say to the theologians and pastors and all the people who ask anxiously 'What's going to happen to the church?': forget the church – think about the kingdom of God, seek its justice and righteousness, and then the living church will be added to you, simply of itself.

First the kingdom of God and then the nation:

We can say to the politicians and ordinary people and everyone who is concerned about the safety of the country, or who is afraid of the power of the state: forget the country or the state – think about the kingdom of God and its justice and righteousness. Then you will keep the power of the state within bounds and make it serve the rights of everyone, and the rights of nature too.

First the kingdom of God and then the economy:

We can say to the entrepreneurs, the trade unionists, the producers, the consumers, and all the people who work to increase the gross national product: forget the profits and forget the growth – think of the kingdom of God and its justice and righteousness. Think of justice for the poor in the countries of the Third World and in the shadows of our Western society. Think of justice for the coming generations for whom we are working. Think of justice for the nature from which we live. Think in the long term, not in the short. Then 'lasting development' will be added to us all, simply of itself.

First the kingdom of God, then our own identity:

We can say to all the people who are worrying about themselves and their own lives, and who are unsure of themselves: Don't withdraw into yourselves. Make your own contribution. Get involved. Only people who find the kingdom of God find themselves. And people who really and truly find themselves find the kingdom of God. For the kingdom of God is within too, very deeply 'within us'. Play your part in God's kingdom and even now, in the present, let something of the rebirth of all things become visible which Christ will complete on his day. Come alive, for your life is coming!

29

II

The Passion of Christ and the
Pain of God

1. Suffering and the question about God

Meaningless, endless suffering, suffering with no way out, makes people cry out for God and despair of God. Faith in God and atheism both have their deepest roots in pain like this. If there is a God, why all this suffering? asks the one. If only there is no God, then there is no problem, says the other. What do we cry out for when we suffer? Some people ask a theoretical question about God: how can God let this happen? They have the impression that God is a blind force of destiny without any feeling, who doesn't trouble himself about anything. For God it is a matter of indifference when children die in Iraq and in the slums of Latin America. He isn't bothered. People get this impression about God because they threaten to become like this themselves – untouched, cold, and indifferent towards suffering. The question: how can God let this happen? is an onlooker's question. It isn't the question which the people involved ask. I look back to July 1943, when I lay under the hail of bombs that rained down on my home town of Hamburg, annihilating 80,000 people in a storm of

30

fire. In what seemed like a miracle, I lived, and I still don't know today why I am not dead too, like my companions. In that hell I didn't ask: why does God let this happen? My question was: my God, where are you? *Where is God?* Is he far away from us, an absentee God in his own heaven? Or is he a sufferer among the sufferers? Does he share in our suffering? Do our sufferings cut him to the heart too? The theoretical question: how can we 'vindicate' God in the face of suffering (the theodicy question) is one thing. The existential question about God's involved companionship in suffering is another. The first question presupposes an apathetic God. The second is looking for a God who suffers with us.

These questions bring us to the heart of the Christian faith: the message of the crucified Christ. In asking them we shall move forward in three steps:

We shall try to 'see' what really happened in Christ's passion. Putting aside our preconceived ideas, we shall try to enter into Christ's experience of God in Gethsemane and on the cross. We shall learn to 'weigh up and judge', asking about the theology of the cross. And we want to act and suffer knowing what we are doing. So we shall ask, finally, about the consolation of the crucified God in our suffering, and about our discipleship of the cross in this world.

2. The passion of Christ

At the centre of the Christian faith is a history: the history of the passion. We have to take this quite literally, in the double sense of the word 'passion'. The history of Christ is the history of a great passion, a passionate love. And just because of that, it became at the same time the history of a deadly agony.

At the centre of the Christian faith is *the passion of the passionate Christ*. The story of the passion has this active and this passive side. In earlier times people often overlooked the passion which drew Christ into his suffering. The Man of Sorrows then became the prototype of dumb submission to a distressing fate. Today on the other hand people like to overlook the suffering which is part of every great passion. They want to be completely, painlessly happy, so they repress suffering. They anaesthetize pain and rob themselves of feeling. Life without passion is a poor thing. Life without the preparedness for suffering is thin and poverty-stricken. The fear of passion has to be got over, just as much as the fear of suffering. Otherwise life cannot be born again. We shall pause at two moments or stages in the story of Christ's passion and ask what happened there: in Gethsemane and on Golgotha.

Gethsemane

The story of Jesus' passion doesn't just begin when he was arrested and tortured by the Roman soldiers. It begins much earlier. It already begins in the province of Galilee, at the moment when Christ resolves to go with his disciples to Jerusalem, the centre of power, injustice and Roman violence. In Jerusalem his passion for the kingdom of God, the healing of the sick, the liberation of the humiliated, the forgiveness of sins, was bound to come up against its most implacable enemies – the collaborators among his own people, and the Roman occupying power. His entry into Jerusalem was triumphant. The people gathered in the streets, crying: 'Hosanna! Blessed is he who comes in the name of the Lord! Blessed is the kingdom of our father David that is coming!' (Mark 11.9f.). It is easy enough to understand the nervousness of the people responsible for law and order, who were afraid of a popular rising. The man from Nazareth was dangerous, so he must disappear swiftly and without more ado.

Now so far there is nothing special about this story. Many

brave men and women, many freedom fighters, have gone to their deaths open-eyed for the sake of their people's liberation. But in Christ's case, something different intervenes, something which is at first quite incomprehensible. In the night before the Romans arrested him, he went to the garden of Gethsemane, taking only three of his friends with him, and 'began to shiver and to quail', as Mark writes. 'He began to be sorrowful and afraid', reports Matthew. In other words he was overcome by despair. 'My soul is very sorrowful, even to death', he says, and begs his friends to stay awake with him.

Earlier too Christ had often withdrawn at night in order to be one with God in prayer. Here for the first time he doesn't want to be alone with God. He seeks the protection of his friends. Protection from whom? And then follows the prayer which sounds like a demand: 'Abba, my Father, all things are possible for you; take this cup from me' (Mark 14.36) – spare me this suffering. What suffering? In Matthew and Luke the prayer sounds somewhat more modest: 'If it be possible' and 'if you are willing' let this cup pass from me.

God, Jesus' Father, did not grant his request. Elsewhere in the New Testament we always hear: 'I and the Father are one.' But here Christ's oneness with God seems to be shattered. That is why Christ's friends fall into a deep sleep, as if numbed by their grief. In this severance Christ only holds fast to his union with the God of his love and his passion through his self-overcoming 'nevertheless': 'Nevertheless, not my will but yours be done.' With Christ's plea in Gethsemane, a plea which was not granted but was rejected through God's silence, his true passion begins: *his suffering from God*. Of course there was also his simple, human fear of pain. It would be cruel to maintain that as Son of God Christ could not have felt any fear. But it would also be foolish to take him for a sensitive weakling, overwhelmed by self-pity at the thought of bodily torment and his approaching death.

I believe that it was a quite different fear which overcame Christ here and tore his soul apart. It was the fear that he, the only-begotten Son, who loved the Father as no one else had ever loved him, could be 'forsaken' by the Father. He didn't fear for his life. He feared for God. He feared for the Father's kingdom, whose happiness he had proclaimed to the poor.

This suffering from God himself was the real torment in Christ's passion. This being abandoned by God was the cup which did not pass him by. The terrible silence of God in response to Christ's prayer in Gethsemane was more than a deathly stillness. Mystics have felt it too, in the dark night of the soul in which everything that makes life living dries up, and hope disappears from life. Martin Buber called it 'the eclipse of God'.

Who can stay awake in this night of God? Who will not be numbed and paralysed by it? Jesus' friends were protected from its terror by a deep sleep. Luke, the doctor, and other witnesses talk about a 'bloody sweat' which fell to the ground from the waking, praying Christ. The Luther Bible heads this chapter 'The Struggle in Gethsemane'. The struggle with whom? Christ's struggle with himself? I think it was more than that. It was Christ's struggle with this experience of God. That was his agony. And he endured the agony through his self-surrender.

Golgotha

The other story comes at the end of Christ's passion, at Golgotha, the place of execution. Again, it is a prayer, or rather: a despairing cry for God. 'And at the ninth hour, Jesus cried out loudly: "My God, my God, why have you forsaken me?"' (Mark 15.34); and then he died with a loud cry.

He hung on the cross for three hours, nailed there, evidently locked in silent agony. And then he died with a cry like this, a cry expressing profoundest abandonment by the God on whom he had set all his hope and for whom he was hanging there on the cross. Historically, this must be the very kernel of what happened on Golgotha. For the notion that the last words of the dying Son to God his Father could possibly have been: 'you have abandoned me' is an idea that could never have taken root in the Christian faith if these terrible words had never been actually uttered, or if their sense, at least, had not been evident in Jesus' death cry. We shall never be able to get used to the fact that at the centre of the Christian faith there is this cry of the God-forsaken Christ for God. We shall always try to soften down its realities, replacing them by more pious last words. We already find this in the New Testament, and afterwards in church history. And yet, terrible though this death cry of Christ's is, we feel obscurely that it is important for us, indeed vitally necessary. For it is the very cry in which so many tortured people can join, because it expresses their true situation: 'My God, why have you forsaken me?'

This saying does not become any more acceptable either just because it is the opening of Ps. 22. The notion that the dying Jesus prayed the whole of Psalm 22 on the cross is surely implausible and far-fetched. For one thing the psalm ends with a glorious prayer of thanksgiving for deliverance from death; and there was no deliverance on the cross. For another, people who were crucified were very soon incapable of speech. No, it is the cry for God of someone who has been abandoned. Early manuscripts of Mark's Gospel put it more drastically still: 'Why have you exposed me to shame?' And 'Why have you cursed me?' Even the very much later Letter to the Hebrews holds fast to this remembrance: that 'far from God' (literally 'without God') 'he tasted death for us all' (2.9). And it is only here, on the cross, that Christ no longer calls God familiarly 'Father', but addresses him quite formally as

'God', as if he felt compelled to doubt whether he *was* the Son of God the Father.

What Christ was afraid of – what he struggled with in Gethsemane – the reason he implored the Father – did not pass him by. It happened on the cross. Christ endured the abandonment by God in which no one can intervene for anyone else, in which everyone is alone, and no one can stand. Is there any answer to the question why God forsook him? The gospel says it was 'for us', for you and for me, so that we should no longer be alone. God delivered up his Son 'for us', so that he could be the Brother of all forsaken people and could bring them to God.

At the centre of Christian faith is the history of Christ's passion. At the centre of this passion is the experience of God of the God-forsaken Christ. Is this the end for every human faith in God, or is it the beginning of that reborn faith which can no longer be shaken by anything at all? The passionately loving Christ, the persecuted Christ, the lonely Christ, the tortured Christ, the Christ who suffers under God's silence – this is our brother, the friend to whom we can entrust everything because he knows everything and has suffered everything that can happen to us, and more even than that. But where is God? If he is simply *not there* in Christ's passion, we should have to say: Christ yes – Christ I can understand, and he understands me. But a God who abandons him – no!

3. The theology of the cross

Christ died with the cry 'My God, why have you forsaken me?'. And every Christian theology tries to offer an answer to this question of Christ's. But is there any real answer? Aren't the Christian theologians often like Job's friends, who want to explain his suffering to him, whereas he is simply not willing

36

to be consoled? Let us look at some of the questions which confront us when we come face to face with Christ's cross and his experience of God-forsakenness.

Why did God abandon Christ on the cross?

We find a first answer in Paul and John. God surrendered Christ 'for us'. He did it out of love for us. Paul argues as follows: The God who raised Christ from the dead is the same God who 'delivered him up' to death on the cross. Out of the forsakenness of the crucified Christ who cries 'my God, why?' Paul already hears the answer: 'He who did not spare his own Son but gave him up for us all, will he not also give us all things with him?' (Rom. 8.32). But was this Christ's own will? Paul says yes, and talks about 'the Son of God' who *gave himself* for me' (Gal. 2.20). So did God sacrifice 'his own Son' and let him die in the pain of the cross alone? Then this God would not merely be an apathetic God. He would be a cruel God too. No, says Paul, for when Christ, God's Son, suffers death, the Father of Jesus Christ suffers the death of his only, his beloved Son. When the Son dies on the cross in God-forsakenness, God the Father also suffers his forsakenness by the Son. So both suffer, though in different ways. Christ suffers the pains of dying, God suffers the death of the Son. So Christ's passion lays hold of God himself too, and becomes God's passion. Paul puts this in the well-known words: 'God was *in* Christ, reconciling the world to himself' (II Cor. 5.19). If God the Father was *in* Christ, the Son, this means that Christ's sufferings are God's sufferings too, and then God too experiences death on the cross. How ought we to imagine this – that God is the one who gives Christ up to death in God-forsakenness, and is yet at the same time the one who *exists and is present* in Christ? Paul has nothing to tell us here. But there is an old Jewish story which can give us a clue to the mystery:

37

When the Holy One, blessed be He, comes to free the children of Israel from their banishment, they will say to him: Lord of the world, it was Thou who first scattered us among the nations, driving us out of our home country; and is it again Thou who now leads us back again? And the Holy One, blessed be He, said to the children of Israel: When I saw that you had left my dwelling place, I left it also, in order that I might return there with you.[1]

God goes with us, God suffers with us. So where Christ, God's Son, goes, the Father goes too. In the self-giving of the Son we discern the self-giving of God. If this were not so, the Gospel of John could not say 'He who sees me sees the Father' (John 14.9). In Christ's God-forsakenness, God goes out of himself, forsakes his heaven and is *in* Christ himself, is there, present, in order to become the God and Father of the forsaken. Christ dies with a cry for God, by whom he feels forsaken. Where is God in what happens on Golgotha? He is *in* the dying Christ. To the question 'why' there are many answers, and none of them adequate. More important is the question 'where'. And for that Christ himself is the answer.

Why did God take this suffering of Christ on himself?

What is the meaning of that terrible happening on Golgotha? To this question there are two answers. First, so that God could be *beside us* in our suffering and with us in our pain. That means: *God's solidarity* with us. Second, so that he could be there *for us* in our guilt, freeing us from its burden. That means: God's *atoning intervention* for us.

1. Solidarity christology: Christ our brother   The Gospels tell the story of Christ's passion as the history of an ever-deeper self-emptying on Christ's part. His male disciples run away when he is taken prisoner by the Romans, one of them betrays him, another denies him – and Christ loses his identity as their Master. The priests of his people surrender him to the Romans – and Christ loses his identity as Jew. Pilate has him tortured and his body destroyed, and orders him to be killed as 'an enemy of the human race' (as 'represented' by the Roman power) – and Christ loses his life. The hymn in the Letter to the Philippians sums up this path of humiliation:

He emptied himself,
taking the form of a servant . . .
he humbled himself
and became obedient unto death,
even death on a cross (Phil. 2.7f.).

If God takes this road with Christ, if God himself was *in* Christ, then Christ brings God's companionship to people who are as humiliated and as emptied of their identity as he was. Christ's cross stands between all the countless crosses which line the paths of the powerful and the violent, from Spartacus to the concentration camps and to the people who have died of hunger or who have 'disappeared' in Latin America.

Christ's sufferings are not exclusive: they are not just his sufferings. They are inclusive – our sufferings too, and the sufferings of the time in which we are living. His cross stands between our crosses, our Brother's cross, as a sign that God himself participates in our suffering and takes our pains on himself. The suffering Son of man is so much one of us that the unnumbered and unnamed, tortured and forsaken human beings are his brothers and sisters. That was the conversion experience of the fifty-nine-year-old Archbishop Romero in San Salvador. 'In the crucified people of history the crucified God became present to him', writes his biographer Jon

39

Sobrino: 'In the eyes of the poor and oppressed of his people he saw the disfigured face of God.'[2]

Christ entered into this humiliation and this forsakenness so that he could become a brother for the humiliated and forsaken, and bring them God's kingdom. He doesn't help through supernatural miracles. He helps by virtue of his own suffering – through his wounds. 'Only the suffering God can help', wrote Dietrich Bonhoeffer in his death cell.[3] God always helps first of all by suffering with us. 'Even in hell you are there.' So no suffering can cut us off from this companionship of the God who suffers with us. The God of Jesus Christ is the God who is on the side of the victims and the sufferers, in solidarity with them.

2. *Atonement christology: Christ the redeemer*   From very early on, the community of Christians saw Christ's passion as the vicarious divine atonement for the sins of the world. Following the model of the Suffering Servant in Isaiah 53, they saw Christ as the divine Son who reconciles through his vicarious suffering. How ought we to understand this? Is atonement necessary at all? I believe it is. In his book *The Sunflower*,[4] Simon Wiesenthal tells that once when he was a prisoner in a concentration camp he was called to the deathbed of someone in the SS; the man wanted to confess to him, the Jew, that he had taken part in mass shootings of Jews, and to ask for his forgiveness. Wiesenthal could listen to the murderer's confession, but he couldn't forgive him; for no human being can forgive a murderer in the name of the dead victims. This story makes it clear that atonement is necessary if someone is to go on living with a burden of guilt like this. Without forgiveness of the guilt, the guilty cannot live, for they have lost all their self-respect. But there is no forgiveness of guilt without atonement. Yet atonement is not possible for human beings, because the wrong that has been done cannot be 'made good'

by any human act. Is atonement for human guilt then possible for God?

In the religions of many peoples, atonement is sought through the sacrifice of animals, sacrifices that are supposed to appease the wrath of the gods which has been roused by human wrong-doing. In Israel it was different. There was a vicarious sacrifice in Israel too – 'the scapegoat', which God gave, so that the sins of the people could be transferred to it through the laying on of hands, and so that the goat could carry these sins out into the desert, away from the people. But the scapegoat is not offered to God in order to appease his wrath. *God gives* the scapegoat in order to reconcile the people. There were similar vicarious sacrificial rites in Solomon's temple too. According to the prophet Isaiah's vision, God will send a new 'Servant of God' who will take away the sins of the people. In the Bible it is always *God himself* who 'carries' the people's sins, and in this way brings about reconciliation. God himself is the one who suffers vicariously 'for us' and 'for many', as our representative. God himself is the atoning God.

How does this happen? It happens because by 'carrying', or 'bearing' human guilt, God transforms it into his own suffering. According to the New Testament, Christ does not only become the Brother of the victims. He becomes the one who atones for the guilty too. 'Thou who bearest the suffering of the world': that is for the victims. 'Thou who bearest the sins of the world': that is for the ones who have committed the wrong. As long as this world endures, God bears not only the world's history of suffering but its history of human wrong and injustice too. In the crucified Christ, God himself is the victim among victims. So it is the victims who testify to the reconciliation of the perpetrators. Victims have a long memory, for the traces of suffering are deeply etched into their souls, and often into their bodies too. The people who have committed the injury always have short memories. They don't know what they have done, and don't want to know. So those who commit acts of violence are dependent on the victims if they want to escape from death into life. The crucified Christ was 'delivered up for our sins' (Rom. 4.25). Earlier, people thought of this as being a sacrifice which Christ makes, or a 'ransom' which he pays, in order to redeem men and women. Nowadays we think of it in personal terms. Christ did not die for individual sins; he died for us sinners. He bears us with our sins by bearing and enduring us. Finally, in being 'for us' Christ makes it plain that 'God is for us' too (Rom. 8.31).

Is God capable of suffering?

If we follow the fashion of Greek philosophy and ask what attributes or characteristics are 'appropriate' for God, differentiation, diversity, movement and suffering all have to be excluded from the divine nature. The divine substance is incapable of suffering; otherwise it would not be divine. The absolute subject of modern philosophy is also incapable of suffering; otherwise it would not be absolute. Impassible, immovable, uncompounded and self-sufficing, the Deity stands over against a moved, suffering, divided and never self-sufficient world. For the divine substance is the founder and sustainer of this world of transitory phenomena; it abides eternally; and so it cannot itself be subjected to this world's destiny.

But if we turn instead to the theological proclamation of Christian tradition, we find at its centre the history of Christ's passion. The Gospels tell us about the sufferings and death of Christ. The self-giving of God's Son for the reconciliation of the world is communicated to us in the eucharist in the form of bread and wine. When Christ's passion is made present to us in word and sacrament, faith is awakened in us – the Christian

42

faith in God. Men and women who believe owe their freedom to Christ's intervening representation. They believe in God for Christ's sake. God himself is involved in the history of Christ's passion. If this were not so, no redeeming effect could radiate from Christ's death. But *in what way* is God himself involved in the history of Christ's passion? If deity cannot suffer, how can Christian faith see Christ's passion as the revelation of what God is? Does God simply let Christ suffer for us, or does God himself suffer for us *in* Christ?

Right down to the present day, the apathy axiom has left a deeper impress on the fundamental concepts of the doctrine of God than has the history of Christ's passion. To be incapable of suffering evidently counts as the irrelinquishable attribute of divine perfection and bliss. But does this not mean that right down to the present day Christian theology has failed to develop a consistently Christian concept of God? And that it has leaned instead on the metaphysical tradition of Greek philosophy?

The ability to identify God with Christ's passion dwindles in proportion to the importance that is given to the apathy axiom in the doctrine of God. If God is incapable of suffering, then logically speaking Christ's passion can only be viewed as a human tragedy. And anyone who can only see in Christ's passion nothing more than the suffering of the good man from Nazareth must inevitably view God as the cold, silent and unloved heavenly power. But that would be the end of the Christian faith.

Christian theology is therefore essentially compelled to perceive God himself in Christ's passion, and to discover Christ's passion in God himself. Numerous attempts have been made to mediate christologically between apathy and passion so as to preserve the apathy axiom; but it would seem more consistent if we simply stopped making the axiom of God's apathy our starting point and started from the axiom of

God's passion instead, so as to understand Christ's suffering as *the passion of the passionate God*. The word passion has the double meaning of suffering and overwhelming feeling and ardour; and because of this double sense, it is extremely well suited to express the central truth of the Christian faith. Christian faith lives from the suffering of a divine passion, and is itself the passion for life which is prepared for suffering. Why did the theology of the patristic church hold fast to the apathy axiom, although Christian devotion adored the crucified Christ as God, and although the Christian proclamation was quite well able to talk about God's suffering? We could give two reasons:

1. God's essential incapacity for suffering distinguishes him from human beings and all other non-divine things, which are subject to suffering as well as to transience and death.

2. If God confers salvation on human beings by giving them a share in his eternal life, then this salvation also confers on human beings immortality, non-transience, and with it the incapacity for suffering too.

Apathy is therefore the very essence of the divine nature, and the purest manifestation of human salvation in communion with God. But logically the argument falls short, because it takes account of only a single alternative: either an essential incapacity for suffering, or a fateful subjection to suffering. But there is another, third form of suffering too: active suffering, the willingness to open oneself to be touched – moved – affected by something other than oneself; and that means the suffering of passionate love. In Christian theology, the apathy axiom really only says that God is not subject to suffering in the same way as transitory beings. So it is not a real axiom at all; it is the statement of a comparison. It does not exclude the possibility that in another way God can certainly suffer, and does suffer. If God were in every respect incapable of suffering, he would also be incapable of love. He would at most be able to love himself, but not anything other than himself. But if he is capable of loving something other than himself, then he opens himself for the suffering which love for the other brings him, while still remaining master of the pain which is the consequence of his love. God does not suffer out of deficiency of being, like created beings. But he does suffer from his love, which is the overflowing superabundance of his being. And in this sense he can suffer.

4. The practice of discipleship of the cross

We must not define 'practice' too narrowly, seeing it merely as what we *do*. The passive experiences which we call suffering belong to the practice of living too. So we shall ask first about the meaning of 'the crucified God' for sufferers in our own time.

The consolation of the crucified God

People who suffer without any reason always think first that they have been abandoned by God and that all the good things in life are in eclipse. People who cry out for God in their suffering can find that they are joining in Christ's death cry. They discover in the suffering Christ the God who understands them and suffers with them. Once we sense this, we perceive that God is not the cold, remote force of destiny whom we have to accuse and cry out against, but that in Christ he has become the human God who cries out with us and in us, and who intervenes on our behalf when torment makes us dumb. The God who has become human has made our lives part of his life, and our sufferings his suffering. That is why when we feel pain we participate in his pain, and when we

45

grieve we share his grief. We are told that Catherine of Siena once cried out: 'My God and Lord, where were you when my heart was plunged in darkness and filth?' And she heard the answer: 'My daughter, did you not feel it? I was in your heart.'

The crucified God helps us. How? Men and women who suffer do not merely protest against fate. They feel the pain because they love life, and because they affirm life they are truly alive. People who no longer love the lives of others and their own lives become apathetic and no longer feel pain. Life and death have become a matter of indifference. They destroy their interest in life through alcohol or drugs. But the more we love, the more vulnerable we are. Love for life makes us capable of happiness. But love for life makes us able to suffer too. The more we can rejoice, the more we can suffer and grieve. That is the dialectic of human life. Love makes life living – and it makes us human beings mortal. We discover the livingness of life and the deadliness of death together and at the same time, through the vested interest in life which we call love.

How can this love for life be born again out of suffering and grief? That is the real question. An almighty God who cannot suffer is poverty-stricken, because he cannot love. Protesting atheists live a life of despair. They suffer because they love, and they protest against the suffering – and against the love which has led them into the suffering. They would like to give back their ticket for this world in which even children suffer. People who believe in the God who suffers with us, recognize their suffering in God, and God in their suffering, and in companionship with him find the strength to remain in love and not to become bitter, in spite of pain and sorrow.

Why God permits all this we do not know. And if we did know, it would not help us to live. But if we discover where God is, and sense his presence in our suffering, then we are at the fountainhead – the source out of which life is born anew.

Anyone who hears the message of the crucified Jesus hears the call to discipleship as well; and anyone who enters into the discipleship of Christ must be prepared to take up the cross. That is what the Gospels already tell us. Christ isn't merely a person. He is a road too. And the person who believes him takes the same road he took. There is no christology without christopraxis, no knowledge of Christ without the practice of Christ. We cannot grasp Christ merely with our heads or our hearts. We come to understand him through a total, all-embracing practice of living; and that means discipleship. In the Reformation period, the Anabaptist Hans Denk put it by saying: 'No one is able verily to know Christ except he follow him in life.' Discipleship is the holistic knowledge of Christ, and for the people involved it has a cognitive as well as an ethical relevance: it means knowing and doing both.

What does the way of Christ consist of? According to the Gospels it means participating in Christ's own messianic passion: 'Go and preach: the kingdom of heaven is at hand. Heal the sick, cleanse lepers, cast out demons. You received without paying, give without pay' (Matt. 10.7f.). These are the very same messianic acts which were supposed to show John the Baptist that Jesus was the promised Christ (Matt. 11.5). Proclaiming God's kingdom to the poor means giving back to them the divine dignity of which the violent have robbed them. Healing the sick means planting the seeds of life in this world of death. Cleansing lepers means accepting the handicapped who are pushed out of our society. Casting out devils means shaking the idols set up in our national and social life, to which so many of the weak have been sacrificed. In other words, men and women who take Christ's road take up the struggle of life against death. And as a result they will get to feel the violence of the powerful, who spread death because

47

they live at other people's cost. So following Christ means engaging in the struggle of life against death, and against the people who spread death. It means engaging in this struggle in our own place and our own time. In my own situation, I see 'the way of Christ' in the struggle against the system of nuclear deterrent and for peace on the foundation of justice; in the struggle against the exploitation and indebtedness of the countries of the Third World; and in the struggle against the deadly destruction of nature.

Christ's messianic passion always puts us on the side of the victims of the violent. That is why discipleship of Christ is marked by a long series of martyrs for faith, life and justice. There are martyrs of faith. They are Christians who are persecuted and killed for their faith. There are martyrs of obedience. They are Christians who are persecuted and killed because of their public activity. And there are martyrs for the kingdom of God and its righteousness and justice. They are people who consciously or unconsciously witness to justice in conditions of injustice. There is the martyrdom of Christians, the martyrdom of the just, and the dumb, collective martyrdom of the sacrificed people.

Whenever the community of Christians remembers the sufferings of Christ, it also remembers the suffering of the martyrs who have participated in the sufferings of Christ. In remembering Christ's sufferings and the sufferings of the martyrs, we remind God himself of his promises, and wait for the future of his kingdom: 'Remember, O Lord, what has befallen us; behold, and see our disgrace . . . Why dost thou forget us for ever, why dost thou so long forsake us?' (Lam. 5.1, 20). If forgetfulness is the order of the day, the dead are slain once more. Painful remembrance preserves hope. Remembrance hastens the redemption.

As I write this I see before me the picture of Brother Juan Ramon Moreno, one of the six Jesuits murdered in El Salvador.

He is lying in a pool of his own blood in Jon Sobrino's room, and in the blood lies my book, which has fallen to the ground: *El Dios Crucificado – The Crucified God*. This chapter is dedicated to his memory.

III

The Anxiety of Christ

1. Fear and hope

One of Grimm's fairy tales tells the story of the boy 'who went out to learn how to be afraid'. He goes through the most perilous adventures completely unimpressed and finding nothing frightening about them. He knows neither dread nor terror. Then one night his wife, who loves him, teaches him what these things mean: she pours a bucket of cold water full of prickly little fish over him as he sleeps; and he is overwhelmed by a nameless horror and abysmal panic in which he feels like a stranger to himself.

Two modern thinkers, one a theologian and one a philosopher, have taken up this story, but they draw very different conclusions from it.

In *The Concept of Dread*, Kierkegaard used the tale as a peg on which to hang his own thesis:

One of Grimm's fairytales is a story about a lad who went out to seek adventure in order to learn how to shiver with fear. We will let the adventurer go his ways without concerning ourselves further about whether he met horror as he went or not. What I should like to say here is that this is

50

an adventure which everyone has to face: the adventure of learning how to be afraid, so as not to be lost, either through not having learnt how to fear, or through being completely engulfed by fear. The person who has learnt how to be afraid in the right way has learnt the most important thing of all.[1]

Ernst Bloch began the foreword to his *Principle of Hope* with the seemingly diametrically opposite thesis:

Once upon a time a man went out in order to learn how to be afraid. That was easier to do in times past, when fear was always close at hand. The art of being afraid was something people were terribly proficient in. But now, except where there is a real reason for fear, a more appropriate feeling is expected of us.

The important thing is to learn how to hope. The labour of hope never gives anything up. Hope is in love with success, not with failure. Hope is higher than fear. It is not passive like fear. Even less is it locked away into pure Nothingness. The emotion of hope goes out of itself. It expands men and women instead of constricting them and hedging them in . . .[2]

Here learning to be afraid and learning to hope are contrasted with one another. But are they really antitheses?

Of course the person who is forced into a tight corner becomes frightened, while hope opens up vision and outlook. Anxiety chokes us. Hope lets us breathe. Anxiety weakens us and makes us small and mean. But people who are strengthened by hope can hold their heads high and learn to walk upright. We are afraid of imprisonment and death. Hope sets its heart on life and liberty. So would it not be better to learn how to hope with Ernst Bloch rather than to learn how to be afraid with Kierkegaard? At first glance everyone would immediately agree that hope is higher than fear. Hope can lead to anxiety, but anxiety can never give us hope. Yet does this simple alternative between anxiety and hope really allow us to grasp the deeper significance of these two attitudes?

What anxiety and hope actually have in common is a sense of what is possible. In anxiety we anticipate possible danger. In hope we anticipate possible deliverance. Of course it is true that in our anxiety we always envisage the worst, and our terrified imaginings increase our anxiety. But without the feeling of fear and anxiety we should simply not notice the danger at all. Without fear we should be blind, ruthless and rash. In anxiety and hope we go beyond existing reality and anticipate the future, so as to make a correct decision about the present. How could we hope for life, liberty and happiness and snatch hopefully at the chances of these things which the future offers, if we did not simultaneously fear death, oppression and misfortune? The future is as ambiguous as potentiality itself. For the world process has not yet been finally decided. Consequently the future means both opportunity and danger. It fills us with enthusiasm, yet at the same time it threatens us. And if this is so, how can we learn to hope without also learning how to be afraid? Even if 'hope is higher than fear' as Bloch says, anxiety is still the inescapable and self-evident sister of hope. We cannot learn to hope if we suppress our anxiety and shut our eyes to danger. But on the other hand we must also ask ourselves whether anyone has ever learnt how to be anxious unless he has first gone out of himself in hope and lived in hope? Can we ever know what anxiety is if we never venture to hope for anything? If we have to learn how to be afraid, as Kierkegaard says, we need an even greater hope if we are not to be numbed by anxiety or totally engulfed by it. When we look towards the open future, dark and undetermined as it is, it is hope that gives us courage; and yet it is anxiety that makes us circumspect and cautious – that gives us foresight. So how can hope become wise without anxiety? Courage without caution is stupid. But caution without courage makes people hesitant and leaden-footed. In this respect 'the concept of dread' and 'the principle of hope' are not opposites at all. They are quite capable of complementing one another.

2. The anxiety of Christ

All human anxiety and fear is fundamentally – which means from birth onwards – fear of separation. Fear makes us lonely. Fear isolates us. Fear strikes us dumb. Do fear and anxiety isolate us from the foundation of our being too, from the meaning of life, from God? Normally the gods know no anxiety, for they exist independent of any changing destiny, in some world beyond life and death, in eternal bliss. Yet if this is what divine eternity is like, then anxiety isolates men and women from their gods too, making their lives completely godless and meaningless. But in this case surely people who can fear and hope because they are capable of love, are greater than all the gods who know neither anxiety nor hope because they cannot love?

If we believe in Christ, fear does not isolate us from God. On the contrary, it leads us deeper into community with him. Christian faith in God is essentially fellowship with Christ, and fellowship with Christ is essentially fellowship with the Christ who was tempted and assailed, who suffered and was forsaken. In our anxiety we participate in Christ's anxiety; for in his suffering Christ went through the very fears and anxieties which men and women encounter too.

Because of this, for Christian devotion the crucified Jesus has always brought consolation in anxiety and fear. And this is certainly not because Christ, as God's Son, was by nature able to live free of anxiety and was incapable of suffering. He is our consolation just because of his 'agony and bloody sweat'. Paul Gerhardt's hymn brings this out particularly vividly:

> And when my heart must languish
> Amidst the final throes,
> Release me from mine anguish
> By thine own pain and woe.[3]

All we have to say as Christians about 'religiously integrated anxiety' and the way to overcome anxiety can be found in this verse. We have to be 'released' from fear. We cannot 'get the better of it' by ourselves. And we are not released from it through the divine omnipotence of a heavenly Christ. We are released through the very contrary: through Christ's earthly and most profoundly human suffering and fear. 'Only the suffering God can help', wrote Bonhoeffer from his prison cell.[4] And Kierkegaard too, after the passage we have quoted, goes on to talk of Christ 'who was in dread even unto death'. But this means that we are released from our fear through Christ's fear, and we are freed from our suffering through Christ's suffering. Paradoxically, these wounds of ours are healed through other wounds, as Isaiah 53 promises of the Servant of God.

3. 'Release us from our anguish . . .'

Whatever pain, weakness and loneliness people experience in their fear of separation culminates in the experience of being forsaken by God. It is this that drives the anxiety which is beyond everything definable and finite, and which therefore threatens our very identity so hellishly. What Christ experienced in his fear in Gethsemane is the crystallization of this measureless anxiety which consciously or unconsciously lies heavy on the hearts of all human beings. He is the most assailed of all, for he suffered anxiety in its godless depths and did not run away from it. He suffered the fear of being forsaken by God which all the rest of us can feel but which we do not really and truly have to endure. People who in their fear have this sense of being forsaken by God experience a 'godly grief' (II Cor. 7.9). They participate in Christ's anxiety because Christ has borne the very same anxiety they feel. In their anxiety they 'conform' to the forsaken Christ. In the image of the crucified Jesus our indefinable anxiety takes on a form with which we can identify, because in that image we discover our own total wretchedness. It is part of ourselves, our own identity, our own grief. This is the conformity christology of the 'Christ with us' – Christ the brother on our road through fear, temptation, captivity, expulsion and expatriation, and abandonment by God. It was this which inspired the Luther renaissance of the 1920s, and through the writings of Jochen Klepper and Heinrich Vogel it saved the souls and lives of many men and women in the fears and anxieties of the Second World War and the post-war years. But this identification between the believer and Christ found its best expression a long time before that, in Paul Gerhardt's great hymn, *Auf, Auf mein Herz*,[5] and it is echoed in many of the passion hymns:

> I feel the life his wounds impart,
> I feel my saviour in my heart.[6]

The other idea, which is inextricably linked with the first, is Christ's vicarious suffering of fear and pain. He suffered for us 'and for many'. He stands in our place. After Easter, whenever Paul and the Epistle to the Hebrews talk about the suffering of

Christ, they never forget to add that interpretative 'for us'. These words bring out the uniqueness and unrepeatability of Christ's suffering and pain. Believers are not just brought into the solidarity with Christ's fate which we have described. They also, and even more, enter into a relationship of gratitude freed from fear. For the knowledge that someone else has gone through everything that threatens me, and which I was afraid of, is for me a liberation. It liberates me from my fear of fear. The knowledge that the suffering Christ intervenes 'for me' and surrenders himself for my sake to the abyss of fear and abandonment by God, frees me from my own anxiety, for it gives me an indestructible identity in him. It 'releases' me from anxiety, so that I can leave it behind me, and its threatening power collapses. But it also frees me to look at my fear squarely and no longer to be afraid of it. That is why gratitude for the fear Christ suffered is a theme of all Christian passion hymns:

> Were the whole realm of nature mine,
> That were an offering far too small.[7]

The two images of Christ belong together. Without the brother in our fears there is no fellowship with Christ; without the redeemer in *his* fear there is no liberation from ours.

If, then, we sum up the experience of faith in anxiety and fear, this is what we can say:

Our countless anxieties continually crystallize in a general fear of life. That fear of life is the heightened, diffused anxiety which grows and spreads, takes on an existence of its own and robs men and women of their self-confidence, indeed of their very identity. It wins the upper hand and drives us into a corner if we fail to identify it for what it is, or if we try to suppress and ignore it. Then we feel that there is no way out of our situation. We no longer know who we really are.

Theology identifies this anxiety as 'God forsakenness'. It is a separation phobia, a dread of severance from the ground of our being, from the meaning of life, from what is worthy of trust. To identify anxiety and put a name to it is not enough to free us from it, or to let us get the better of it. Even 'religiously integrated anxiety' still does not mean that our anxiety is abolished. We have to be 'released' from it. That is the experience of faith in anxiety. In the remembrance of Christ's anxiety and fear, what he has already done with us and for us is actualized and repeated: he endured the fear of being forsaken by God – that fear of separation we have talked about – and he has struck out a way through this experience for those who trust and follow him. In fellowship with him we discover that we are released from fear as we endure it. By recognizing our fear in his, and by seeing our fear as caught up into his, we experience that 'blessed anxiety' (as Georges Bernanos called it) which kindles an unconquerable hope. To be released from fear means getting up out of fear and resisting it. It means walking freely through the midst of it.

IV

The Tortured Christ

It was twenty-two years before Jean Amery was able to write about it: in 1943 he had been taken prisoner and tortured by the SS in Belgium. They bound his hands together behind his back and pulled them up until his arms dislocated, and then flogged him, seemingly for ever. He wrote: 'No one looks beyond this into a world where the principle of hope prevails.' And a few years after he had written these words he committed suicide. What he wrote is true. In the hell of the torture that destroys body and soul and shatters the personality, there is no hope. That is why Dante sets over the entrance to hell: 'Abandon hope all ye who enter here.' The same words might be written over every human torture chamber. No one comes out of it whole. No one comes out of it the same. Not the person tortured, and the torturer even less.

1. What makes people torture?

Religious motives

I used to think that torture was simply motivated by personal sadism, or terrorism, or war, in which people stick at nothing. But the more I looked into the matter, the more deeply I was horrified by the religious motives which impel many torturers.

In the Iranian revolution under Khomeini it was said that the guardians of the revolution were actually supposed to torture and destroy the bodies of their enemies, because they believed they were the enemies of God, and that this was the way to save their souls. A film set in the Second World War showed an Australian prisoner-of-war who had stolen a chicken from the Japanese commander and was nailed to a door and flogged; this was supposed to be necessary in order to purify his sinful soul. We find the same ideas in the Bible too: 'If you beat him with the rod you will save his life from Sheol' (Prov. 23.14). 'It is better that you lose one of your members than that your whole body be thrown into hell' (Matt. 5.30). The apostle Paul wanted someone in the congregation in Corinth to be 'delivered to Satan for the destruction of the flesh, that his spirit may be saved in the day of the Lord Jesus' (I Cor. 5.5).

Let us go a step further and look at the notions about hell and its tortures which grew up in Christianity and Islam; for hell is nothing other than religion's torture chamber. Biblical dictionaries define hell as the place 'where the Devil and the damned have to suffer eternal torment (= torture)'. According to Cyril, one of the church Fathers, hell is the land of death where there is no life; the realm of darkness where there is no light; an abyss out of which the groans of the damned rise up without there being anyone to listen and pity them; a pit out of which they miserably cry 'woe', but find no one willing to be moved by their plight; a place they all implore but no one hears their plea; where they are all forsaken and have no comforter. 'There all the senses are tortured', explains Gottfried Büchner's *Hand-Konkordanz* (1750, 29th ed. 1927): 'sight through eternal darkness, hearing through weeping and the gnashing of teeth, smell through the stink of sulphur, taste through the bitterness of eternal death, feeling through eternal torment.' This torture has no end. This fire is inextinguishable. From this hell no one ever returns.

For Tertullian, another Father of the church, the screams of the damned in the fiery pit actually increase the joy of the faithful in heaven – an idea which can still be found in eighteenth-century dogmatics. This is a Christian dream of revenge: the heathen exulted when the Christian martyrs died in torment in the arena, and in heaven Christians will exult when, in return, the heathen are tormented in hell.

We can all see in our mind's eye the apocalyptic pleasure with which the torments of unbelievers in hell are depicted in mediaeval paintings. Earthly torture chambers are finite, and bodily torment ends sometime or other, with death. But cruel apocalyptic fantasy knows no limits. This torture is supposed to endure eternally. No death can release the damned. The fire of the hellish pyres burns inextinguishably.

In the world of the imagination the two kinds of torture lent force to one another. Earthly torture was supposed to anticipate the eternal tortures of hell, thereby averting them; and the eternal tortures of hell were thought to justify earthly torture. The hellish pains of torture which apocalyptic lust thought out for unbelievers and the godless are a prototype for all the ways of 'making life hell' for other people. What seems to me particularly infamous here is not that the body is tormented so that the soul may be saved, but that both bodily anguish in the fire and spiritual anguish in the divine judgment are always described in every detail: enmity ends apocalyptically with the annihilation of all one's enemies, not with the conquest of their enmity through love, as in Jesus' Sermon on the Mount.

Anyone who is against torture and protests when 'life is made hell' for other people must get rid of this apocalyptic friend-enemy thinking. As long as there is a hell for God's enemies – and ours – in religion, there will also be direct and indirect justifications for torture chambers on earth.

Judicial motives

On the next level we find the religious justification of torture in the form of expiatory penal law, and in the imposition of punishment as a deterrent. In expiatory penal law, suffering equivalent to the wrong committed is inflicted on the wrongdoer: an eye for an eye, a tooth for a tooth. Evil is repaid by evil. And this has nothing to do with the wrongdoer personally. It is a matter of the divine world order, which has been infringed and now has to be restored through expiation. The punishment of wrongdoers accomplishes something that is cosmically important. They are punished in what for them is valuable and precious. This used to be their bodies. In modern European times it is their liberty. That is why corporal punishment has been replaced by imprisonment – deprivation of freedom.

Anyone who has suffered a long period of imprisonment knows how loss of freedom too is a punishment that can destroy a person, psychologically and even physically. Because expiation used to have cosmic dimensions (since it restored the divine order of the world), punishments were public. They were originally thought of, not as a popular entertainment, but as a kind of open-air service in which the people participated, as a way of conciliating the deity and putting heaven in a propitious mood.

Deterrence is always an element in expiatory criminal law, and it used to take the form of the public torture of criminals. Public torture was supposed to deter potential wrongdoers. But when it was inflicted on conquered peoples, it was also designed to suppress political and social rebellion. It was a method of public terrorization of the subjugated. The Roman cross on which Christ publicly died was an instrument of torture used to punish rebels against the *pax romana*, and slaves who had risen against their masters. After the Spartacus revolt, the Via Appia was lined by seven thousand crosses with dying slaves. The public mass executions carried out by the German occupying power in the Second World War were also designed to terrorize the subjugated people. The infringements of human rights in the Balkans are the most recent example of this kind of torture, torture used in retaliation and as a deterrent.

Anyone who wants to take a stand against torture and have it abolished will also have to abandon an expiatory criminal law, and the notion of punishment as a deterrent.

Secular motives

Does the end justify the means? In German one even asks: does the end *sanctify* the means, showing that there is still a religious element in this thinking, even if here we are at the furthest limits of what can be called religion. Is it permissible in wartime to torture prisoners in order to extort information from them? Is this merely a question of weighing up one thing against another, if the information is vital for me and my own cause? Or are there absolute limits which can never, ever be crossed whatever the circumstances? Is there any end which justifies the means of torture, or does torture as means discredit every end to such an extent that it can no longer be an end at all for human beings? Many people – and by no means just soldiers and policemen – will point to exceptional situations which justify the use of torture for the sake of getting information.

But can any country permit its ends to be sullied through the use of torture without losing its self-respect? Ends justified by the means of torture are unjustifiable; they are no longer ends worth living for. Every country needs this self-respect, because its political legitimation depends on it. The Germany in whose name the Nazis used the cruelest tortures for twelve long years lost all its lustre in our eyes. A country that uses torture cannot be a 'fatherland'.

But if a country's glory radiates from its constitution, and if its value rests on the human dignity and human rights it guarantees, that country cannot permit torture, not even in extreme situations. Even if in some individual case everything would seem to speak in its favour, here we come up against a limit which is absolute, because here the foundation of the constitutional democratic state is infringed. A soldier or policeman who tortures other people in the name of his country is destroying that country, not protecting it.

Personal motives

Some of the people who are employed to torture, and some who are prepared to torture, are evidently driven by a perverted motivation: sadism, a sensual pleasure in rape, delight in inflicting pain, and the intoxication of power at being able to break other people by forcing one's will on them. It is obvious that the chance of tormenting other people will attract sadists.

But not all the guards in the concentration camps in Nazi Germany were sadists who derived active, lustful pleasure from torturing defenceless prisoners. Much worse, apparently, were the men and women who were completely lacking in any emotion at all, who were simply 'doing their duty', as they put it, and 'faithfully carrying out orders'. The professional mechanism with which people were systematically tortured and murdered is perhaps even more horrifying than the perverted sadism, because it can take hold of every one of us once our personal conscience has been suspended, or once we have surrendered it to some other authority.

Anyone who enters the lists against torture and wants to have it abolished must see to it that the sadists are not given a chance, and that the power of personal conscience is stronger than the compulsion 'to obey orders' or than the 'force of circumstances' which we hear so much about.

2. The tortured Christ is the brother of the tortured

At the centre of the Christian faith is the history of a passion: the history of the betrayed, denied, tortured and crucified Christ. No other religion has a martyred figure at its centre. This has evoked revulsion among many aesthetes, from Cicero to Goethe. But among feeling men and women it has evoked sympathy too. The helplessness and forsakenness of Christ awakens our compassion, just like the helpless baby in the manger. What does the torture of Christ have to say about torture in general? Does his torture justify torture by Christians, or the torture of the enemies of Christianity, either here on earth or – even more – afterwards in hell? Or does the tortured Christ mean the end of torture, because he is the end of every possible justification of torture, whether it be religious or secular?

'And Pilate had Jesus scourged', says the passion narrative laconically in Matthew, Mark and John. The commentaries tell us: 'Scourging was one of the most severe punishments among the Jews. The evil-doer was tied naked to a pillar and one of the court's ushers flogged him as hard as he could with a curved scourge. Among the Jews the number of blows was not allowed to exceed thirty-nine. Among the Romans there was no limit.' What was the purpose of scourging someone before he was executed? Apparently the aim was to break the victim's physical and mental resistance – perhaps also to shorten his death agony by weakening him beforehand.

64

The evangelists tell the story of Christ's passion in detail, but never with masochistic pleasure over the history of someone's suffering, and never in order to arouse sympathy. They tell it as *God's* history: God with us – with us in our suffering and our torment; and God for us – for us in our guilt. They talk about the solidarity of God-become-human – his solidarity with us until death – and about the representation of the God who intervenes on our behalf.

As we saw in the last chapter, in his passion Christ stripped himself of all his human relationships, and seemingly of his relationship to God as well. 'He emptied himself', says the Letter to the Philippians. Betrayed, denied and left alone by the men who had been his disciples; crucified by the Romans as an enemy of the state, and indeed of the human race; forsaken by God on the cross – so divested, he arrives at the point of our own most profound desolation. If this Christ is not just one human being among others – if he is the messiah, Israel's deliverer and the redeemer of men and women – then his history is first of all an expression of God's solidarity with the victims of violence and torture. Christ's cross stands between the countless crosses set up by the powerful and the violent throughout history, down to the present day. It stood in the concentration camps, and stands today in Latin America and in the Balkans, and among those tortured by hunger in Africa. His suffering doesn't rob the suffering of these others of its dignity. He is among them as their brother, as a sign that God shares in our suffering and takes our pain on himself. Among all the un-numbered and un-named tortured men and women, that 'Suffering Servant of God' is always to be found. They are his companions in his suffering, because he has become their companion in theirs. The tortured Christ looks at us with the eyes of tortured men and women.

Of course not every tortured person feels this subjectively, not even every tortured Christian. Of course 'the dark night of

65

the soul' is to be found too in the torture chambers and the isolation cells, that night where all bearings are lost and every feeling dries up. But objectively the tortured Christ is present in the tortured, and the God-forsaken Christ in the God-forsaken.

This brings us back to the question of hell. The Apostles' Creed runs: 'He descended into hell, on the third day he rose again from the dead . . .' When did Christ suffer hell, and how? An early interpretation says that he endured hell after he died, when he descended to the underworld of the dead, in order to proclaim to them the gospel of their redemption. Luther said that Christ went through hell in the days of his death, in the time between Gethsemane and Golgotha, when he experienced the bitterness of having been forsaken by God. The two interpretations complement one another:

– The betrayed, forsaken, tortured, lonely Christ, who died in fear, experienced in his own body and his own soul what we call hell.
– The Christ who comes to the dead brings the dead deliverance. This Christ has risen into eternal life. So not only is death swallowed up in the victory of life; hell too is cheated of its victory.

Since Christ descended into hell, what we experience as hell, and everything else that can be called hell, has been objectively transformed. Now there is someone who has brought hope into hell. Dante is confuted. There is someone who has thrown hell open and led out the dead, as we see him doing in every Orthodox Easter icon. If hell was the place of God-forsakenness, ever since Christ's descent into hell it has been this no more. If in hell the devilish spirits of torment rule over human beings, ever since the resurrection of the dead Christ they have been robbed of their victory. 'I am told to believe in hell', said Berdyaev once, 'but not that there is anybody in it.'

Let me say this: Because Christ was in hell, no one who is in hell is without hope any more. But this means that for Christian faith hell is no longer what it was once supposed to be – religion's everlasting torture chamber. Its gates are open. Its walls have been broken down. In hell the trumpet signalling liberation has already been heard. The person who sticks to Christ has no need to fear hell, nor can that person ever threaten others with the tortures of hell. If anyone thinks that for biblical reasons we still have to talk about hell, believers will answer: 'O hell, where is thy victory? But thanks be to God who gives us the victory through our Lord Jesus Christ' (I Cor. 15.55, 57).

3. The risen Christ is the judge of the torturers

Torture used to be demonstratively public, and the bodies of the tortured were left lying as a deterrent. Today torture is secret; it takes place *in camera*, and the bodies 'disappear'. They are buried or burnt, so that no one can find any trace of them and remember their names. No one must come back to accuse the murderers. That is why it is so difficult to follow up clues to the missing in Argentina and Chile. Even earlier, at the end of the war, Himmler had the concentration camp victims dug up again so that their bodies could be burnt. Every trace of them was to be wiped out.

Resurrection also means: the dead return, those who have gone rise again, the nameless are called by their names. That is judgment. Ultimately the murderers will not triumph over their victims, and the torturers will be called to account. Even people who no longer believe in a personal God have this yearning for justice, and understand that resurrection means

67

that the dead will receive the justice that is their due. For Christians, the risen Christ is the forerunner of the raising of the dead. So he is also the beginning of the divine judgment on the torturers and the murderers.

It is understandable that the victims and their children and grandchildren should say that after Auschwitz it is impossible to talk about God any more. But for the evil-doers and for their children and grandchildren the fact is that after Auschwitz God *must* be talked about, because the people responsible are subject to his judgment. Anyone who at this point declares that 'God is dead' is trying to escape their own responsibility. God brings justice to those who suffer violence. God judges those who have committed violence. There is no other way of arriving at a peaceful world in which there is no more torture. It is obvious that no one can forgive a guilty person in the name of his dead victims. It also became clear to us that a past of this kind can never be 'made good'. In order to live with a burden of guilt like this, expiation is needed. Without forgiveness of guilt the guilty who recognize their guilt cannot live, for they have lost all their self-respect. Yet we have seen that there is no forgiveness of guilt without atonement. And we saw too that atonement is not possible for human beings, since no one can atone for injustice like this. Is atonement then possible for God? we asked. And turned for an answer to the cross of Christ.

Through his passion and his death on the cross, Christ put himself on the side of the victims and became their brother. But he did more. He also became the one who atones for the guilty. 'Thou who bearest the sins of the world, have mercy upon us.' It is this prayer which brings us together with the evildoers and within the divine compassion. Compassion is love that overcomes its own hurt, love that bears the suffering which guilt has caused, and yet holds fast to the beloved.

Victims, we said, have a long memory, for they still carry the unforgettable scars of their suffering. Those who caused that suffering have short memories. They don't know what they have done and don't want to know. So the perpetrators are dependent on the victims if they want to turn away from death and enter into life. No expiation can be offered to the victims; the wrongdoers can at most participate in initiatives which are a symbol of expiation, as a way of regaining their self-respect.

If the judge of the torturers is called Christ, then these torturers are confronted by someone who has been tortured. That is the moment of truth. The mask falls. The torturer recognizes himself for what he is. That is judgment. If the judge of the torturers is called Christ, then they are confronted by the one 'who bears the sins of the world'. That is the moment of justice, the justice which creates new life.

4. Resistance against torture

What can *we* do for torturers? If we are honest we have to say: really nothing at all. We can silently leave them to themselves, and to God's wrath. We can point out to them that their divine judge is Christ, whom they have tortured and murdered in their victims. And we can include them in the prayer: 'Thou who bearest the sins of the world, have mercy upon us.' We have to leave them to God, and cannot play God ourselves, either for evil or for good. We have no right either to condemn them or to forgive them.

When there is injustice and torture on a mass scale, and if no alternative is in sight, both the victims and the perpetrators soon get used to the situation. How can we escape from the apathy which is our cultural sickness?

I always became painfully aware of the barbed wire round the prisoner-of-war camp when a transport left to go home.

Then we smelled a whiff of liberty, and it made us totally ill. When freedom is near the chains begin to chafe. When our interest in life is awakened we begin to protest against the powers of death. When once we feel the hunger and thirst for righteousness and justice we are no longer prepared to accept injustice; we fight against it.

So let us strengthen the will for life, our own life and the lives of other people and other created beings. Then the forces that resist torture will awaken too. Let us spread the hunger and thirst for righteousness and justice. Then the injustice will be felt as injustice, and will be manifest as such, and will be ended. Let us take as our example the courage and endurance of the mothers on the Plaza de Mayo in Buenos Aires, who stuck it out there for months in protest and in fear for their missing children; who refused to allow them to be forgotten, but demanded justice.

V

The Resurrection of Christ – Hope
for the World

'If Christ is not risen then our preaching is in vain and
your faith is in vain' (I Cor. 15.14). With these strong
words Paul underlines the fundamental significance of
Christ's resurrection for Christian faith. The Christian faith
stands or falls with Christ's resurrection, because it was
by raising him from the dead that God made Jesus the
Christ and revealed himself as 'the Father of Jesus Christ'.
At this point belief in God and the acknowledgment of
Christ coincide; and ever since, for Christian faith the two
have been inseparable.

Christians believe in Jesus for God's sake, and in God for
Jesus' sake. Anyone who draws a dividing line between belief
in God and acknowledgment of Christ doesn't know what the
Christian faith is about. Christian faith in God is faith in the
resurrection. It is only the pictures and symbols which have
anything to do with the mythical world picture of Christianity's early period. In our experience belief in the resurrection is confronted and challenged by death, the fate to which
everything living is subjected. Faith in the resurrection is the
faith in God of lovers and the dying, the suffering and the

71

grieving. It is the great hope which consoles us and gives us new courage.

This being so, it is a pity that there should be Christians who no doubt believe in a God, but not in Christ's resurrection. For them, Jesus turns into a historical personality who in the process of time sinks further and further into the historical past. From this liberal reduction of Jesus to the past history we can read about in the textbooks, it is only a short step to Islam. 'God yes, but Jesus no' is not a Christian option.

On the other hand there are Christians who for various theoretical or personal reasons feel that God doesn't mean a thing to them, but who still have a certain feeling for 'the man from Nazareth'. This is 'the Jesus of the atheists', the Jesus of the existentialist Albert Camus and the Marxist Milan Machovec. But then why does it have to be just Jesus who is important for humanity? Why not Buddha, Socrates and Gandhi too? 'God no, Jesus yes' is not a Christian option either.

So let us try out another approach, attempting to interpret faith in God and the confession of Christ mutually. We shall begin by looking at the early Christian accounts of the resurrection. Then we shall turn to the modern question about history and the resurrection, seeing what we are permitted to hope for, and what we ought to do. In the third section we shall step outside that paradigm of the modern world whose name is history, and shall move into the paradigm of the post-modern world – into an ecological understanding of history and nature, human history and the history of the earth. We shall ask about the future of the earth in the light of Christ's resurrection, and for this purpose we shall once more take up the patristic church's doctrine of physical redemption, so as to arrive at a new understanding of Christ's bodily nature and our own.

1. The special character of the resurrection faith

Jesus was crucified publicly and died publicly. But the only people to learn of his resurrection were the faithful women at his tomb in Jerusalem, and the disciples who had fled into Galilee. The disciples then returned to Jerusalem and proclaimed the crucified Jesus quite openly as the Lord and redeemer of the world, whom God had raised from the dead. Those are the relatively well-attested historical facts. And they are astonishing enough. But at the same time, all that can actually be proved about them are the assurances of the women that at Jesus' empty tomb they heard an angelic message telling them of his resurrection, and the assertions of the disciples that they had seen appearances of Christ in Galilee.

Apparently after Jesus' death many of his men and women disciples experienced a great many manifestations in which Jesus allowed himself to be seen as the Christ, who is eternally alive in God. In the earliest testimony to the resurrection we have, in the First Letter to the Corinthians, written in the year 55 or 56, Paul cites testimonies that Christ had appeared to Cephas, to the twelve, and then to five hundred brethren at once. At the end he adds himself. Paul's account is especially valuable because it is a personal record of what he himself experienced when Christ appeared to him. According to what he says, Paul 'saw' Jesus, the Lord (I Cor. 9.1), but this 'seeing' evidently took the form of an inward experience: 'It pleased God through his grace to reveal his Son *in* me' (Gal. 1.15f.). The appearance was something that happened to him unexpectedly and completely against his will, for he was a rabbi and had actually been commissioned to persecute Christians in the synagogues. 'I was seized by Christ', he says (Phil. 3.12), and this experience turned his life upside down.

We ought probably to imagine the women's experience of

Christ at the tomb, and the disciples' experience in Galilee, as being not very different from this – if it is possible to enter imaginatively into exceptional visions of this kind at all. The witnesses all agree in reporting that they saw Jesus – the Jesus who had died – as 'the living One'. They all say that he is alive in that eternal glory of God in which he then 'appeared' to them in their earthly lives. They had visions of a supernatural light.

But at this point the interpretations already begin. It is in any case impossible to filter out the substance of these experiences in the form of naked facts detached from their subjective human interpretation. All that would emerge would be unhistorical abstractions. Pure facts are in any case unstatable. In every perception, what is experienced is interpreted with the help of ideas which the people concerned bring with them. Of course these ideas themselves are changed in the process of the perception. And in the case of experiences which turn one's world upside down, this is true to a particular degree. Otherwise Saul could never have become Paul. The experiences of Christ which are being talked about here were apparently experiences which changed the whole of existence. In their disappointment and fear, Jesus' former disciples had fled from Jerusalem to Galilee in order to save their lives; because of these experiences, these same ex-disciples became apostles who returned to Jerusalem and risked their lives there in order to proclaim Christ 'boldly'.

Because the visionary phenomena were evidently linked with ecstatic experiences of the Spirit, they will also have passed into the pentecostal experiences of the early church, and will have continued there: the perception of Christ's presence in his appearances led on to the experience of Christ's presence in the Spirit. The early Christian faith in the resurrection was not based solely on Christ's appearances; it was at least equally strongly moved by the experience of God's

Spirit. Paul therefore calls this divine Spirit 'the life-giving Spirit' or 'the power of the resurrection'. Believing in the risen Christ means being seized by the Spirit of the resurrection.

Paul interprets the christophany which he experienced with the word *apocalypsis*, and by doing so he gives the experience a special meaning: God reveals ahead of time something that is still hidden and inaccessible to the ways of arriving at knowledge which are at our disposal in the present aeon, or world time. 'The mysteries of the End-time' and of God's future new world are veiled and impenetrable under our present conditions of knowledge, because the present world of sin and violence cannot sustain the new world of God's justice and righteousness. So this divine justice and righteousness will create the present world afresh. The christophanies were not interpreted as being mystical translations into a world beyond this one. They were seen as the advance radiance of God's coming glory which will shine on the first day of the new world's creation (II Cor. 4.6). Moreover they are all daylight visions, not dream visions in the night.

If we look at the way these christophanies and Easter visions were interpretatively perceived by the people concerned, we see that their structure has three different dimensions:

1. They were *prospective* visions of hope: the men and women saw the crucified Jesus as the living Christ in the splendour cast ahead by God's coming glory.

2. They were *retrospective* visions of remembrance: the disciples recognized Jesus from the marks of the nails and from the way he broke the bread. The One who will come is the One crucified on Golgotha.

3. They were *personal call* visions: the men and women concerned perceived in this 'seeing' their own call to apostleship: 'As the Father has sent me, even so I send you.'

2. The resurrection in the perspective of history

It is one thing to see Christ's resurrection in the perspective of history. That inevitably brings us up against the question: is this a historical event or an interpretation of faith? But it is another thing to see history in the perspective of Christ's resurrection. Then the question facing us is the eschatological one – the question, that is, about the end of this world's history of suffering, and the world's new creation.

History: the modern paradigm

In the seventeenth century, the concept of 'history' began to develop, as an all-embracing paradigm for interpreting human beings and nature, God and the world. In the human project of scientific and technological civilization, harmonizations with the laws of the cosmos and the earth were replaced by blueprints plotting progress from an old and obsolete time – the past – into the new time of the future. The more European domination over other peoples was pushed forward, and the more human beings subjugated nature, the more the rich multiplicity of cultural groups gave way to the unity of humanity. That great singular 'History' was born.

It was in the framework of this paradigm 'history' that the modern science of historical studies also came into being. The historical criticism of legends of rule in church and state developed, and with it the historical awareness which sets the presence in tradition of what is past at a temporal distance, so that the past can be historicized and the present freed from the previous decisions and previous judgments of tradition. 'The true criticism of dogma is its history', said David Friedrich Strauss,[1] and made the historian the ideological critic of religious dogmas and political legends. In historical awareness, events of the past are transformed into past events.

If we look at Christ's resurrection from the standpoint of this modern paradigm 'history', using the categories of the modern historical mind, then – in spite of all the disputes – it makes no great difference whether we see the resurrection as a product of the disciples' imagination, or view it as a historical fact; for as a past event that is becoming ever-more-past and ever-more-remote, Christ's resurrection can neither determine the present nor have any relevance for the future. The modern category 'history' has already turned the happening into something past and gone; for anything historical is something that comes to pass, and then passes away.

Ernst Troeltsch certainly no longer has the last word today, even among historians, but his treatise on 'Historical and Dogmatic Method in Theology' (1898)[2] had classic importance for the theology of the resurrection in the twentieth century. Troeltsch transferred scientific methods to historical studies and named four axioms for the critical historical method as a way of arriving at soundly established knowledge. We shall put Christ's resurrection to the question by confronting it with these axioms.

1. Historical research can never do more than arrive at assessments based on probability. It can never achieve absolute knowledge. Can theology base the assurance of faith on assessments of historical probability? No.

2. There are interactions between all phenomena in historical life. They are the ontological foundation – the basis in existence – for the connections between cause and effect which apply everywhere. Is Christ's resurrection an exception, and a breach of natural law? No.

3. We can only arrive at historical understanding if we take analogy as our guideline. 'The almighty power of analogy' is based on the homogeneity of all historical happening. Can an event that has no analogy, such as Christ's resurrection, be understood in historical terms? No.

4. Objective historical knowledge, then, is subject to the principles of probability, correlation and analogy. These principles assume that history is made by human beings, not by any obscure powers, gods and demons, and that history can consequently also be *known* by human beings. Can we talk in a modern historical sense about the activity of a transcendent God in history generally, and about God's raising of Christ in particular? No.

If these principles determining history and historical studies are valid, then Christian theology is brought up against the fundamental question: in what category can it talk about God and Christ's resurrection at all? Troeltsch himself already complained about the schizophrenia of Christians in the modern world, for whom there was a Sunday causality in which God rules and determines history, and an everyday causality, in which all happening has its immanent, this-worldly cause. Can a new 'public' theology get over this split consciousness? Or must theology detach itself from the sense of truth publicly and generally shared in modern society, in order to stand by its own truth?

The horizon of expectation and the space of experience

Historical studies do not just have history as their own object of research. They themselves are embedded in history and are part of it. So historical methods and categories have to be fitted into the metahistorical concepts and categories on which they are based. History means interaction and process between people, between human groups, classes and societies, between human beings and nature, and – not least – between human beings and what they consider to be the Absolute.

There is history as long as there is time. Time is perceived only as long as the difference between past and future exists.

The difference between past and future is determined in the present presence of both – the presence of the past in remembrance, the presence of the future in hope. It is the difference between 'the space of experience' and 'the horizon of expectation' which determines the awareness of historical time. If there are no longer any expectations of future experiences, then the remembrance of past experiences fades and slips away from us too. If there are no longer any remembered experiences, then there are no expectations either. Remembrance and hope are the conditions for experiencing history. So they are also the conditions for an interest in history, and a concern about it. To experience reality as history presupposes hope for its future. Hope for the future is grounded on remembrance.

So let us look at the fundamental difference between expectation and experience, so as to unfold history in the perspective of Christ's resurrection. 'The resurrection of Christ' is a meaningful postulate only if its framework is the history which the resurrection itself throws open: the history of the liberation of human beings and nature from the power of death. In the framework of history defined in any other way, the resurrection of Christ is not a meaningful postulate at all.

3. History in the perspective of the resurrection

When we talk about Christ's resurrection from the dead we are not talking about a fact. We are talking about a process. We are talking in one and the same breath about the foundation, the future and the practical exercise of God's liberation of men and women, and his redemption of the world. So what we can *know* historically about Christ's resurrection must not be abstracted from the question of what we can *hope* from it, and what we have to *do* in its name. Kant made this intrinsic connection clear. It is only in the living unity of knowing, hoping and doing that Christ's resurrection can be understood in its true historical sense.

To see history in the perspective of the resurrection means participating through the Spirit in the process of the resurrection. Believing in the resurrection does not just mean assenting to a dogma and noting a historical fact. It means participating in this creative act of God's. If it were merely a historical circumstance, we should simply say: 'oh really?', register the fact, and go on living as we did before. But if it is a creative act of God's, then – if we really know and understand what it is about – we shall be born again to a new life. A faith like this is the beginning of freedom.

If God reveals himself in the resurrection of the Christ crucified in helplessness, then God is not the quintessence of power, as this was represented by the Roman Caesar; nor is he the quintessence of laws, as these are reflected in the Greek cosmos. God is the life-giving energy which makes the poor rich and lifts up the downtrodden and raises the dead. Faith in the resurrection is itself an energy which strengthens and raises people up, liberating them from the deadly illusions of power and 'having', in the perspective of life's future. The proclamation of Christ's resurrection is a meaningful statement against the horizon of the history which it itself throws open: the history of the liberation of human beings and the whole sighing creation from the powers of annihilation and death.

Understood as a confronting event which discloses the future and opens up history, Christ's resurrection is the foundation and promise of eternal life in the midst of this history of death. Paul established this connection quite definitely and explicitly: 'If the Spirit of him who has raised Jesus from the dead dwells in you, he who has raised Christ Jesus from the dead will give life to your mortal bodies also through

the power of his Spirit which dwells in you' (Rom. 8.11). He
links the perfect tense of Christ's resurrection with the present
tense of the indwelling of the Spirit, and the present tense of
the Spirit with the future tense of the resurrection of the
dead. The raising of Christ is not a phrase describing a past
happening. It is the name for a confronting event in the past
which in the Spirit determines the present because it opens up
the future of eternal life. The present-tense liberating experience of the Spirit is grounded on the perfect tense of Christ's
resurrection; while the future 'giving life to mortal bodies'
(which is the way Paul describes the resurrection of the dead in
this passage) has its objective foundation in Christ's resurrection and is perceived through the experience of 'the life-giving
Spirit'. So in talking about Christ's resurrection we have to talk
about a *process* of resurrection. This process has its foundation
in Christ, its dynamic in the Spirit, and its future in the true
new creation of all things. Resurrection doesn't mean a closed
fact. It means a way: the transition from death to life. But what
life does this mean?

The formulation about 'giving life to mortal bodies' shows
that the resurrection hope isn't concerned with another life. It
has to do with the fact that this mortal life here is going to be
different. Resurrection is not a consoling opium, soothing us
with the promise of a better world in the hereafter. It is the
energy for a rebirth of this life. The hope doesn't point to
another world. It is focussed on the redemption of this one. In
the Spirit, resurrection is not merely expected. It is already
experienced. Resurrection happens every day. In love we
experience many deaths and many resurrections. We experience resurrection through the rebirth to living hope. We
experience resurrection through the love which already brings
us to life here and now; and we experience resurrection
through liberation: 'Where the Spirit of the Lord is, there is
freedom' (II Cor. 3.17).

Because it is the beginning of the annihilation of death and the appearance of eternal life, the raising of Christ from the dead is 'the fact that changes everything', so it is in itself the revelation of God. As 'the Wholly Other', God is the radical criticism of this world, as Karl Barth said. As 'the One who changes everything', God is the Creator of the new world. The resurrection faith itself is already a resurrection in the energy of life. The resurrection of Christ qualifies world history, making it end-history, and sets the spaces and sectors where we experience history against the horizon of expectation of the new creation.

4. Resurrection in the perspective of nature

With the beginning of modern times, the historicity of Christ's resurrection became theology's central problem, because 'history' had become the modern world's great paradigm. By history, people meant the history of human beings, as distinct from nature. Consequently a distinction was made between the humanities and the natural sciences. Nature was supposed to be the realm of necessity, history the realm of freedom. This dichotomy meant that the spirit was thought of as something outside nature, while nature was supposed to be devoid of spirit. Only medicine wavered between the humanities and the sciences. It was not until the beginning of the nineteenth century that in Europe it was finally assigned to the sciences. So are human beings nothing but nature? Aren't they spirit too?

Because every woman and every man is a unity of body and soul, spirit and nature being inextricably interwoven in their existence, the fundamental modern distinction between history and nature cannot be completely sustained. The paradigm 'history' does not take in the whole of reality; it splits up its wholeness. So we must go beyond this modern paradigm and develop a new one which will grasp nature *and* spirit, history *and* nature, as a unity, and will integrate what has been divided.

If we look at Christ's resurrection from this standpoint, we can see that we shall have to transpose modern 'historical' christology, or understanding of Christ, into a new *ecological* christology. This ecological christology brings us back to the patristic church's christological doctrine of the two natures, as a way of integrating nature, because we see that there can be no redemption for human beings without a redemption of the whole of perishable nature. So it is not enough to see Christ's resurrection merely as 'God's eschatological act in history'. We also have to understand it as *the first act in the new creation of the world*. Christ's resurrection is not just a historical event. It is a cosmic event too, as the Orthodox Easter liturgy and our ancient Easter hymns have always known. We have to grasp this cosmic dimension of Christ's resurrection in a new way.

Is the expression 'the raising of Christ' adequate? It is taken from Jewish apocalyptic, and is an eschatological symbol – a symbol that has to do with the end which God will bring about. Here God is the active agent – the 'doer of the deed' – and the dead Jesus is passive. Does the other phrase 'Christ's resurrection' take us any further? Logically, the theological symbol of the divine 'raising' is balanced by the anthropological symbol of the human 'resurrection': the person who has been woken has to get up. Otherwise the waking has no effect. According to the symbol of raising, the dynamic comes from above; according to the symbol of resurrection it comes from below. Christ was not merely raised up by God. He himself rose.

Are these two symbols, taken together, sufficient for us to comprehend the mystery of Jesus? Both are metaphors for actions, either on God's part or by Jesus. But there are metaphors from nature as well describing what happened to the crucified and dead Jesus. The first is the image of Christ's 'rebirth' from the eternal Spirit of God: through the eternal Spirit Christ offered himself for us (Heb. 9.14), through the Spirit he was 'born again' to eternal life (I Cor. 15.45).

For this Paul uses the nature image about the grain of wheat: 'It is sown corruptible; it is raised incorruptible' (I Cor. 15.42 AV). It is only when the grain of wheat falls into the ground and dies there, that it brings much fruit, says John (12.24), meaning Christ's death and resurrection. According to the Letter to the Colossians, Christ is 'the first-born from the dead' (1.18). So we can complement the apocalyptic symbols of God's raising and Christ's rising through the symbol of Christ's 'rebirth' from the eternal divine Spirit. The Orthodox icons make this clear: Christ was born of Mary in a cave hollowed out of the earth; out of a grave in the earth he was born again to eternal life through the Spirit. With Christ's rebirth, the rebirth of the whole cosmos begins, not just the rebirth of human beings (Matt. 19.28). His dying and his 'coming alive again' represent a transition, a transformation, a transfiguration, not a total breach and a radical new beginning.

What images should we use to describe the cosmic significance of Christ's rebirth from the divine Spirit? Images from the life of nature. Of course that does not turn Christ's rebirth into a natural phenomenon, as it might be in cellular physiology; for the symbol says that he is reborn to immortal life, not to mortal life. But eternal life is life as well, and rebirth is a birth too. And this makes mortal and natural life open for analogy – and also capable of analogy.

From earliest times, the Christian church has celebrated Christ's resurrection and the festival of the spring together, so that ever since these early times we in Europe have talked about 'Easter'. And it was at the beginning of summer that the church celebrated the experience of the Holy Spirit. The natural analogies from nature were discovered in the morning of the day, the springtime of the year, and the birth of life. So the celebration of Christ's resurrection was joined with joy over the rebirth of nature and the delight of all created beings. Morning, springtime and birth were lifted out of the natural rhythm of nature's growth and decay, its becoming and dying, and were given so enhanced a value that Christ's resurrection meant hope for the redemption of the whole of mortal nature, through the new creation of all things for eternal life.

In the perspective of human history the raising of Christ *from the dead* means that the general raising of all the dead has begun. But that is only the personal side of the hope. In the perspective of nature, the raising of Christ means that the destructive power of death, which is anti-God, is driven out of creation. Death is 'destroyed' (I Cor. 15.26), and in the new creation there will be no more death. That is the cosmic side of the hope.

What experience of life springs from the resurrection hope? The imaginations of hope always open up the way and experience of life, and also restrict it. If someone hopes for the resurrection of the dead and the new creation in which death will be no more, that person will be possessed by the Spirit of the resurrection and will already experience now 'the powers of the world to come'. That person will be 'born again' to a living hope, to take the phrase used from earliest Christian times.

Because resurrection means the whole human being, body and soul, this living hope must already be a hope for the soul and for the body here and now. But that means that it is confronted by death's negation of everything that lives. The Christian faith maintains that it is impossible to bring life and death into harmony with one another without the resurrection hope. Ought we to accept death as a natural part of life? If so we must do without love, for love desires life, not death.

Ought we to renounce the body because it is mortal? If so it would be better not to live at all, for what has never lived can never die either.

But if we affirm life because we love it, we expose ourselves to the pains of death. We can be disappointed and hurt and sad. It is the hope for the annihilation of death and for the resurrection to eternal life which makes us ready to love this life here in such a way that we become vulnerable, mortal and sad. We already experience the power of the resurrection now in love: 'We have passed out of death into life because we love the brethren', says I John 3.14 – and we add 'the sisters' too. In the Spirit of the resurrection hope, love can be as strong as death, because in love the victory of life over death is already experienced.

Death thrusts into this life as the violence of separation. The resurrection thrusts into this life as the power of union, and abolishes what death can do. We can experience this not just in relation to other people. We can experience it in relation to our own bodies too. Plato says that in looking forward to the death of the body, the soul elevates itself above the body and distances itself from its needs and frailties. The knowledge that we are going to die already splits human beings into soul and body in this life, and makes the soul try to dominate and repress the body because, after all, it is ultimately of no more value than the corpse buried in the ground.

But hope for what German bluntly calls 'the resurrection of the flesh' leads to a totally different experience of the body. The *whole* human being, soul and body, is related to the divine, not just the soul; for 'male and female he created them', says the creation account. So it is not just the soul which is to be 'the temple of the Holy Spirit'. It is the body too, as Paul always stresses. But the Holy Spirit is the Spirit of life. Where the Spirit is experienced as present, the body and the soul become a unity once more. The divisions hostile to life and the conflicts

86

addicted to death are overcome. When the fear of death dies, the fear of life disappears too.

In the image of the resurrection of the body, life and death can be brought into harmony in such a way that death doesn't have to be repressed either. In this Spirit of the resurrection I can here and now wholly live, wholly love and wholly die, for I know with certainty that I shall wholly rise again. In this hope I can love all created things, for I know that none of them will be lost.

VI

The Cosmic Christ

1. Christ after Chernobyl

The cosmic interpretation of Christ's death and resurrection took us beyond the bounds of a christology or understanding of Christ in the framework of history, and led us to an interpretation in the framework of nature. Unless nature is healed and saved, human beings cannot ultimately be healed and saved either, for human beings are natural beings. So if we are concerned about the things of Christ, we have to go beyond the christology or teaching about Christ developed in modern times, in which Christ is seen in the context of history. The task facing us now is to develop a christology of nature. When we turn to the New Testament, we find that the doctrine of Christ put forward in the letters to the Ephesians and Colossians is a *cosmic* christology. But, like the patristic church's doctrine of the two natures, this was dismissed by modern Western European theology as mere mythology and speculation. Anthropocentric christology fitted better into the modern paradigm 'history'. But without meaning it, this anthropocentric christology actually became one factor in the modern destruction of nature; for the modern reduction of salvation to the salvation of the soul, or to authentic human existence, unconsciously abandoned nature to its disastrous exploitation by human beings. It is only a growing awareness of the deadly ecological catastrophes in the world of nature which has led to a recognition of the limitations of the modern paradigm 'history', and has prompted us to turn back, and ask again about the wisdom of ancient cosmic christology and its doctrine of physical redemption.

But nowadays there is a difference. In the ancient world, cosmic christology confronted Christ the redeemer with a world of powers, spirits and gods. The proclamation of 'universal reconciliation' freed believers from their fear of the world and from their terror of demons. Today a cosmic christology has to confront Christ the redeemer with a nature which human beings have plunged into chaos, infected with poisonous waste and condemned to universal death, so that he can save men and women from their despair and nature from annihilation. Where is Christ after Chernobyl?

We are only discovering today, and slowly at that, what Chernobyl really means: 8,000 to 10,000 dead; more than 50,000 people fatally contaminated; Chernobyl's children handicapped and born for an early death; a third of White Russia and parts of the Ukraine uninhabitable and shut off. The costs are proliferating indefinitely and incalculably. How long will this go on? The half-life of plutonium is 24,000 years! In those earlier times the theme was 'Christ and cosmos'. Today it is 'Christ and chaos'. The subject of realistic discussion is no longer 'Christ and the forces of the stars'. The subject that concerns us now is Christ and the nature which has been reduced to a rubbish heap. The modern era has given birth to the age of ecological catastrophes. A new cosmic christology must end the historical christology of modern times, not abolishing it but gathering it into something more, which will overcome its limitations and preserve its truth. This is imperative if faith is to discover the therapeutic powers of Christ in the world's present situation, and if we are to make these powers experiencable.

Early on, the churches of the West made a distinction between nature and grace which resulted in a contempt for nature which had fateful consequences, leading first to the modern subjugation of nature and then, in our own day, to its destruction. As long ago as 1961, at the General Assembly of the World Council of Churches in New Delhi, Joseph Sittler gave a moving address[1] in which he pleaded for a return to the cosmic vision of Christ found in the Epistle to the Colossians, and a retreat from the dualism of nature and grace: 'The man of the Enlightenment could penetrate the realm of nature, and to all intents and purposes take it as his sphere of sovereignty, because grace had either ignored this sector or rejected it. And with every new conquest of nature a piece of God died; the sphere of grace diminished to the degree in which structures and processes in nature were claimed by the now autonomous human being . . . Men strut blasphemously about this wounded and threatened world as if it were their own property.' We are therefore living in a moment of crisis, a particular moment or kairos in which Christ and chaos meet, and we must confront the threat to nature with a 'christology of nature', in which the power of redemption does not stop short at the hearts of men and women and their morals, but gathers in nature as a whole. Nature is the scene of grace and the sphere of redemption just as much as history. A christology which is expanded to its cosmic dimensions will kindle a passion for the threatened earth.

2. The cosmic Christ and early Christian tradition

In Paul's own epistles we already find him touching on the cosmic Christ when he is talking about Christ's mediation in creation. In I Cor. 8.6 he says: 'For us there is only one God, the Father, *from whom* are all things and *for whom* we exist, and one Lord, Jesus Christ, *through whom* are all things and *through whom* we exist.' If all things are 'from' God the creator, and 'through' Christ the Lord, then Christ is here interpreted as 'the creator-mediator' and identified with the Wisdom who was beside God *before* the creation of this world and *through* whom God made all things (Prov. 8). The knowledge that Christ was the mediator in creation gave Christians the freedom to live everywhere in the lordship of Christ; they no longer needed to pay any attention to the idols of this world (I Cor. 8.1–13). For Paul, the lordship of the risen Christ who is present in the life-giving Spirit is for God's sake universal in its trend, and knows no other gods or lords beside. The pre-Pauline hymn in the Epistle to the Philippians already praises this universal lordship of the exalted Christ (Phil. 2.9–11). The missionary preaching in the Acts of the Apostles, especially Paul's Areopagus address (Acts 17.22–31), proclaims Christ in universal, cosmic dimensions. Unlike the preaching addressed to the Jews, early Christian preaching to the Gentiles is universalist in what it says about creation and the resurrection of the dead. Here Christ is hardly presented as Israel's messiah at all any more. He is now rather humanity's 'new Adam'. And God is not so much the God of Israel's patriarchs as the creator of the universe 'in whom we live and move and have our being' (Acts 17.28).

The foundation for a knowledge of the cosmic Christ 'through whom are all things' is, as I believe, the Easter experience of the risen Jesus. What was 'seen' there goes beyond all historical remembrances and experiences, and touches the innermost constitution of creation itself. According to Rom. 4.17, resurrection and creation are closely linked. The God who raises the dead is the same God who as creator calls into being the things that are not; and the God who called the world into existence out of nothing is the God who raises the dead. Beginning and end, creation and resurrection, belong together and must not be separated from one another; for the glorification of creation through the raising of the dead is creation's perfecting, and creation is aligned towards the resurrection of the dead. The statements about creation do not 'serve' statements about redemption, and redemption is not merely 'the restoration' of the creation whose original order has become deranged.

The light of the resurrection appearances, then, was already identified very early on with the light that shone on the first day of the new creation; and if this is so, then the Christ who appeared in this light as the first in the resurrection of the dead is also 'the first-born of all creation' (Col. 1.15). 'First' does not mean the first created being in the numerical sense; it means 'the image of the invisible God' who 'is before all creation, and in whom all things hold together' (Col. 1.15, 17). According to Heb. 1.3, this first-born of creation is 'the brightness of his glory and the express image of his person, upholding the universe by his word of power' (Heb. 1.3). The same thing is said about the divine Logos in John 1.1–13. This is a reference to the Wisdom Messiah through whom and for whom God has created all things. According to Prov. 8, Wisdom is God's 'comrade in creation'. She is not yet called first-born, but she is 'before all things, from eternity' (Ecclus. 1.4). All things owe their existence to her, for they have come into being through her mediation. The creator 'makes fast' the universe through the immanent presence of his Wisdom in all things. The Christ who in his resurrection from the dead annihilates death also manifests himself in the dimensions of this creation Wisdom; and he was already understood in this sense very early on.

The practical result was that in the multi-religious cities of the ancient world the Christian community no longer came forward as yet one more religion devoted to a hitherto unknown deity. Instead it acted as the peace-giving and unifying community of the Creator and Reconciler of all things. Its missionary task was not to enter into a competitive religious struggle. Its purpose was to integrate people into the reconciliation and peace which was the eschatological, or ultimate, horizon of the cosmos. The Christ proclaimed to the people of other religions – 'the Gentiles' – is 'the Christ *in us*, the hope of glory' (Col. 1.27), and according to the Letters to the Ephesians and Colossians, this hope means the expectation of the cosmic Christ through whom heaven and earth and all things will find peace.

The church therefore has to be seen as the beginning of the reconciled cosmos which has arrived at peace. It is the historical microcosm for the macrocosm which has become God's temple. But it is the cosmic dimensions of the church that are meant here; the aim is not the churchifying of the world. As 'the body of Christ', the church is always already *the church of the whole creation*. It points away from itself to the glory of God which fills heaven and earth: 'The Most High does not dwell in houses made with hands; as the prophet says, "Heaven is my throne, and earth is my footstool. What house will you build for me, says the Lord, or what is the place of my rest? Did not my hand make all these things?"' (Acts 7.48–50, following Isa. 66.1f.). God is to be adored and worshipped in the temple of his creation: that is the meaning of every church and every cathedral built by human hands. It is only as the church of the whole creation that the Christian community is anything more than a sect or a religious society. If God is not worshipped in creation, he is not properly known in the church either. The true church of Christ is the healing beginning of a healed creation in the midst of a sick world.

3. An outline for a differentiated cosmic christology

Hitherto, cosmic christology has shared the one-sidedness of the traditional doctrine of creation. That is to say, it understands by creation only creation-in-the-beginning, not continuous creation as well, and not the consummated new creation of all things. Creation and redemption then cleave apart and become two separate things. Either creation is down-graded into a preparation for redemption, or redemption is reduced to the restoration of creation-in-the-beginning. In order to acquire a comprehensive concept of creation, we have talked about a unified creation process, which begins with creation-in-the-beginning, continues in the history of creation, and will be perfected in the new creation of all things. In a similar way we shall interpret Christ's mediation in creation in three separate strands or movements:

1. Christ as the ground of the creation of all things (creation-in-the-beginning);

2. Christ as the driving power in the evolution of creation (continuous creation); and

3. Christ as the redeemer of the whole creation process (the new creation).

By proceeding in this way we are really doing no more than taking up the old Protestant doctrine about Christ's threefold kingly office, developing it in the context of today's recognition: Christ rules in the realm of nature, in the realm of grace, and in the realm of glory.

This integral viewpoint makes it possible for us to avoid the one-sided stresses which have hitherto hampered cosmic christology. If Christ is described only as the ground of creation, this world, which is often so chaotic, is enhanced in a way which is really illusory, for it is transfigured into a harmony and a home. If Christ is described solely as the *Evolutor* (Teilhard de Chardin's term), the evolutionary process itself takes on redemptive meaning for the initial creation; but the myriads of faulty developments and the victims of this process fall hopelessly by the wayside. If, finally, we look solely at the coming Christ who is to redeem the world, we see only this world in its need of redemption, and lose sight of the goodness of the Creator and the traces of his beauty in all things.

Creation through the Spirit and the Word

If all things are created by one God, then a transcendent unity precedes their diversity and their historicity. It is not a matter of many worlds belonging to many gods or powers. This is *the one* creation of *the one* God. If all things are created by the one God *through* his Wisdom/Logos, and if they are held together in that, then an *immanent unity* in which they all exist together underlies their diversity in space and time. Their unity is not the outcome of some subsequent process, emerging from their relationships and the warp and weft into which they are bound. Everything has its genesis in a fundamental underlying unity, which is called God's Wisdom, Spirit or Word. The fellowship of all created beings goes ahead of their differentiations and the specific forms given to them, and this is consequently the foundation underlying their diversity. If God withdraws this foundation, everything disintegrates and becomes a nothingness. If God lends it fresh force, the various forms are renewed (Ps. 104.29f.). The Jewish and Christian doctrines about Wisdom or the Logos as mediator in creation are in direct contradiction to the atomist theory put forward by Democritus. The beginning was not the particles. The beginning was the symmetry, the concord. 'The elementary particles embody the symmetries', says Heisenberg: 'They are its simplest representations, but they are merely a result of the symmetries.'[2] Jewish and Christian

95

doctrines of creation have therefore always maintained the idea of nature as a unity.

If we look back at the creation story told in the Priestly Writing, we find the immanent unity of creation expressed in two formulas:

1. In the formula of *creation through the divine Word*: 'God said, "Let there be light"; and there was light' (Gen. 1.3).

2. In the *presupposition* for creation through the Word (a presupposition which has received too little notice), and that is: *the vibration of the Spirit of God present in creation*: 'The Spirit of God hovered over the face of the waters' (Gen. 1.2). The Hebrew word *ruach* is often translated Spirit, as it is here; but a better translation is 'wind' or 'breath'. The Hebrew word *rahaph* is generally rendered 'hover' or 'brood'. But according to Deut. 32.11 and Jer. 23.9 it really means vibrating, quivering, moving and exciting. If this is correct, then we shouldn't just think of the image of a fluttering or brooding dove. We should think of the fundamental resonances of music out of which sounds and rhythms emerge. So in thinking about 'creation through the Word', we shouldn't think primarily in metaphors of command and obedience. A better image is *the song of creation*. The word names, differentiates and appraises. But the breath is the same in all the words, and binds the words together. So the Creator differentiates his creatures through his creative Word and joins them through his Spirit, who is the sustainer of all his words. In the quickening breath and through the form-giving word, the Creator sings out his creatures in the sounds and rhythms in which he has his joy and his good pleasure. That is why there is something like *a cosmic liturgy* and a music of the spheres.

> Sleeps a song in everything
> That is dreaming still unheard.

And the world begins to sing
If you find the magic word.[3]

The securing of creation

The second thing to be said about mediation in creation is that it has to do with its *securing* and preservation. This idea carries us forward from creation-in-the-beginning to continuous creation. 'The preservation of the world' can be understood to mean that God sustains what he has created and watches over the world once he has created it, in order to preserve it from the chaos by which it is unremittingly threatened. But the securing of the world can also be understood as continuous creation. Every instant, the creative God reiterates his primal 'yes' to what he has created. But both these conceptions are related to creation-in-the-beginning, so they are one-sided; they do not permit us to think forward to the consummation of creation. Neither idea about the preservation of creation expresses a positive relationship to the redemption of all things. The realm of grace is cut off both from the realm of nature and from the realm of glory, without any relation to either. But this obscures the grace which is already shown in the preserving and sustaining of creation, in spite of human sin and cosmic disorder.

God preserves his creation from corruption because, and inasmuch as, he has patience with those he has created. His patience creates time for them. His longsuffering leaves them space. His patience, which is prepared to suffer, and his waiting forbearance are the virtues of his hope for the turning back and homecoming to the kingdom of his glory of the beings he has created. The God who preserves the world endures the self-isolation of created beings and puts up with their contradictions, keeping their future open for them through his suffering and his silence, and conceding them the opportunities for conversion which they neglect. God's preservation of the world doesn't belong only to the realm of nature. It is already part of the realm of grace. In the preservation of the world, nature and grace are so closely interwoven that it is impossible to talk about the one without talking about the other.

The renewal of creation

If we think about the preservation of the world in the context of the future, then continuous creation doesn't just mean that the original creation is secure because God holds it fast. Continuous creation is already at the same time *the anticipation of the new creation* of all things. Continuous creation is creation's ongoing history. In this 'historical' creation God 'renews the face of the earth' (Ps. 104.30), looking towards the final new creation of all things. He creates justice for those who have never known justice. He raises up the humble and obscure. He fulfils his promises in historical experiences.

The divine creative and redeeming activity which men and women experience in this way has its hidden correspondences in the world of nature. What we see in the world of nature is not merely God's activity as preserver; we see his activity as innovator too. The history of nature displays the evolution of species as well as their preservation. Continuous *and* contingent happening characterizes the historical process of the natural world, as well as the world of human beings. So even in the history of nature we can discover parables and true symbols for the future of creation as it will be completed and perfected. In nature's preservation and development, God already prepares the consummation of his creation, because his grace thrusts forward to the revelation of his glory. Paul perceives this in imprisoned nature's 'sighing' and 'yearning' for liberty in God's glory. The men and women who experience 'the first fruits of the Spirit' in faith, recognize the same longing of the Spirit as the driving force and torment in everything. The mediators of creation – the Spirit and the Word – wait and strive in everything for the liberation of all things. So 'creation in chains' isn't merely in need of redemption. It is also consumed by hunger and thirst for the righteousness of God.

4. Christ – the driving force of evolution?

It was Teilhard de Chardin especially who interpreted the continuation and completion of creation through Christ with ideas taken from the theory of evolution. In fact to a considerable degree he identified the two processes. For him, the cosmic Christ is 'the Christ of evolution'.

Evolution's driving force

Teilhard took up the vision of the cosmic Christ from the Epistle to the Colossians, his intention being to expand the church's one-sided presentation of Christ as redeemer through the universal perfecter of creation whom he called 'the evolver Christ' or *Christus evolutor*. If the Christian doctrine of redemption is related purely to original sin, it offers no perspectives for the completion and perfecting of creation through a gathering together of all things under the head, Christ, and through their entry into that fullness of God which will one day be 'all in all'. But Teilhard discovered 'the creative side of redemption', and saw this discovery as the step forward to a new theology. The completion of creation in the divine unification is higher than the redemption of the world from its sins, and is redemption's goal. According to Teilhard,

Christ the redeemer 'is fulfilled, without this in any way detracting from his suffering aspect, in the dynamic plenitude of a *Christ the Evolver*'.[4]

In the interests of this view, Teilhard transferred salvation history as Christian faith has understood it to the history of life and the cosmos, understanding this history of nature as an evolution from the simple to the complex, from what is individual to what is shared, from the lifeless to the living, and then to ever more complex forms of living awareness. For Teilhard, salvation history and the evolution of life coincided. He saw the appearance of human beings in the framework of the evolution of life in general. Human beings are the organic continuation of that growth into a particular role which has gone on in the realm of the living – the biosphere – ever since life began, and which already shows itself in the organization of matter itself. With human beings a new phase of life begins, for human beings are reflective, conscious beings. 'We are carried along by an advancing wave of consciousness.'[5] What comes into being is what the language of evolutionary theory calls 'the noosphere'.

But where, then, is the development of human awareness leading? Teilhard used Nietzsche's words about the 'super-man' and the growth of a 'super-consciousness', and said that – in analogy to the forms of organization found at the other stages of evolution – the compression of the many leads to an evolutionary leap into a new quality. A new form of organization is evolving which will one day lift humanity into the sphere of 'the ultrahuman' – i.e.: 'The ultra-human perfection which neo-humanism envisages for Evolution will coincide in concrete terms with the climax which all Christians expect under the concept "incarnation."'[6] The completion of evolution in this transcendent sphere corresponds to 'the fulfilment of God' in the visible world. For the 'divinization' of the world is simply the reverse side of God's incarnation – his becoming human – and vice versa. United, self-transcending humanity ends in God, while at the same time God 'incarnates himself' in the process of this development.

By incarnation Teilhard understood a process which is not exhausted in the one, unique historical person of Jesus of Nazareth, but which strives towards the 'Christification' of the whole cosmos. Because he understood the reality of the world in terms of evolution, he saw this processual incarnation of God 'as coming from what is in front of us'. It is not God in heaven who saves his fallen earth; it is 'le dieu en avant' – the God ahead – who lends the cosmos its impulse towards completion, because he desires to draw everything to himself and into his own fullness. The incarnation of God in Christ should be understood as the beginning of a new phase of humanity, and hence as a new phase in the evolution of life in general. Christ is the beginning of the divinization of humanity, and this divinization will also bring with it the deification of the cosmos; for in this cosmic Christ the becoming-human of the universe and the becoming-human of God converge. If the process of the humanization of the earth and the humanization of humanity is thought through to the end, we discover at the peak of the anthropogenesis – the coming into being of humanity – that final goal and focus of the consciousness which Teilhard calls the Omega Point. 'Is this not now the ideal place from which the Christ whom we worship can radiate?', he asks, and answers: 'Evolution preserves Christ (by making him possible), and at the same time Christ preserves evolution (by making it specific and desirable)'.[7]

But in his firm faith in progress Teilhard seems to have overlooked the ambiguity of evolution itself, so that he fails to pay any attention to evolution's victims. Evolution always means *selection*. Many living things are sacrificed in order that 'the fittest' – which means the most effective and the most adaptable – may survive. In this way higher and increasingly complex life systems undoubtedly emerge, systems which are able to react to changed environments. But in the same process milliards of living things fall by the wayside and disappear into evolution's rubbish bin. Evolution is not just a constructive affair on nature's part. It is a cruel one too. It is a kind of biological execution of the Last Judgment on the weak, the sick and 'the unfit'. If men and women adopt the same way of doing things, what we very soon have is 'euthanasia' – 'the killing of valueless life'. So Teilhard can never have taught 'universal reconciliation' in any form whatsoever, for that contradicts the whole idea of evolution.

When the first atomic bomb was dropped on Hiroshima on 6 August 1945, Teilhard was filled with enthusiastic admiration for the scientific and technological advance which this achievement of a scientific super-brain acting in teamwork had brought humanity. He believed that the control of atomic power would promote the evolution of humanity and the human consciousness in a way never known before. Here Teilhard gave no thought to Hiroshima's hundred thousand dead and the people who are still dying today from radiation damage. He took a purely positive view of the hydrogen bomb tests on Bikini too: 'For all their military trappings, the recent explosions at Bikini herald the birth into the world of a Mankind both inwardly and outwardly pacified. They proclaim the coming of the *Spirit of the Earth*.'[8] Trusting in 'life's planetary instinct for survival', he loftily brushed aside the possibility that humanity could ever suffer a nuclear catastrophe: 'The earth is more likely to stop turning than is Mankind, as a whole, likely to stop *organizing and unifying* itself.'[9] He was incapable of recognizing the possibility of an atomic apocalypse (although Günter Anders, Albert Schweitzer and Karl Jaspers were already talking about this even in 1958), because his confidence in the world made him incapable of considering humanity as a whole to be mortal.

102

For Teilhard, the perspectives of evolution were evidently so vast that while he was no doubt able to join together the remotest points of their beginning and their goal, he found it difficult to perceive what was nearer home. 'We still have several million years in front of us', he wrote from Peking in 1941, thinking of the stage of evolution next to be reached in the socialization and totalization of humanity. He failed to see that time is running out; for the ecological catastrophes which this very socialization and humanization are producing could quite well put an abrupt end to any further evolution at all on humanity's part.

The victims of evolution and their redeemer

Is it conceivable that this future of creation will be purposefully and finally achieved by way of evolution or self-transcendence? No. It is not conceivable, because the process of creation takes place in time, and 'becoming' inevitably involves transience. There is no evolution without selection. Of course we can point out that all the lower forms of life are still inherently present in life's higher forms. But this is true only of *the form*; it is not true of its individual examples, and it does not lead to their immortality. Even the individual contribution to the evolution of the whole brings the individual no eternity. A perfect being as the end of evolution is certainly conceivable, but not the perfecting of all created things.

The perfecting of the whole creation, extended over time in the creation process, is only conceivable *eschatologically* – as the end, that is to say, which God himself brings about. Eschatology is not the end of the evolutionary process. What is eschatological is the new creation of all things which were, and which are, and which will be. What is eschatological is the bringing back of all things out of their past, and the gathering

103

of them into the kingdom of glory. What is eschatological is the raising of the body and the whole of nature. What is eschatological is that eternity of the new creation which all things in time will simultaneously experience when time ends. To put it simply: God forgets nothing that he has created. Nothing is lost to him. He will restore it all.

We have to give the name 'eschatological' to the movement of *redemption*, which actually runs counter to evolution. If we want to put it in temporal terms: this is a movement which runs from the future to the past, not from the past to the future. It is the divine tempest of the new creation, which sweeps out of God's future over history's fields of the dead, waking and gathering every last created being. The raising of the dead, the gathering in of the victims and the seeking of the lost bring a redemption of the world which no evolution can ever achieve. This redemption therefore includes the redemption of evolution itself, in all its ambiguity. In this redemption, evolution turns and becomes re-volution, in the original sense of the word. The linear time of evolution will be carried over into a unique and then final eschatological cycle: into the return of all the pasts in the eternal aeon of the new creation of all things. We have to understand the eschatological future *diachronically*: it is simultaneous to all the times, so it represents eternity for all things.

Teilhard's *Christus evolutor* is the *Christ in his becoming*. But the *Christus redemptor* – the redeeming Christ – is *Christ in his coming*. Walter Benjamin discerned the difference between the two categories with particular sensitivity: 'It is only the Messiah himself who will fulfil all historical happening, and he will do so in the sense that it is only he himself who will redeem, complete and create its relation to the messianic perspective. That is why nothing that is historical can ever of its own volition strive to relate itself to what is messianic. That is why the kingdom of God is not the *telos* of the historical dynamic; it cannot be made the goal. For historically it is not a goal; it is the end.'[10] Yet Benjamin detected a dialectical relationship between the purposeful 'dynamic of the profane' and that other direction, 'messianic intensity': 'The profane is therefore certainly not a category of the kingdom, but it is a category, and the most appropriate category, of its stealthiest approach.'[11] The forces of messianic intensity act in a counter-movement to the coming of the messianic kingdom. And in this way they strengthen one another mutually.

In the context of the cosmic christology we are thinking about, this means that it is only the reconciliation of all things, on earth as in heaven (Col. 1.20), and their redemption from the fetters of the transience of the times which leads to the gathering together of all things in the messiah, and therefore to the completion of creation. The evolutionary series in the history of nature and in human history are the outcome of *continuous creation*. The redemption and the new creation of all created things can be expected only from *the coming of Christ in glory*. The renewal of the cosmos presupposes the resurrection of the dead, for the cosmic Christ will not only become the Lord who fills all spaces of creation with 'the messianic intensity' of the divine peace (shalom). He will also become the Lord who fills all the times of creation with the full messianic *extensity* of redemption. In the Epistle to the Colossians, the spatial picture of the cosmic Christ is dominant; in Paul it is the temporal picture of the eschatological Christ (I Cor. 15). The two images complement one another and it is only together that they can comprehend the risen and exalted Christ in his spatial and temporal dimensions: his 'messianic intensity' pervades the spaces of creation to their depths; his 'messianic extensity' pervades the times of creation to their furthest origins.

This universal eschatology of redemption is the foundation which makes it justifiable for us then to discern and acknowledge tendencies in the evolution of nature and in human history as being also parables and hints, anticipations and preparations for the coming of the messianic new creation. The active self-transcendence which is at work in these processes really does point beyond the historical present and beyond history itself, reaching forward to a future which will fill it and bring it to rest. But the hunger for this future is not in itself this future's realization. The 'absolute self-communication of God' about which Karl Rahner speaks is *heralded* in the radical self-transcendence, but no more than that; it is not itself already the other, divine side of this human self-movement. It is only as a whole that creation will be reconciled, redeemed and recreated. Without the redemption of nature and the raising of the dead, human self-transcendence into the divine life, even if this succeeds, remains a fragment. At best it is a glimmer of hope for this unredeemed world.

5. Political and spiritual consequences

Some people think that concern about our ruined environment is a worry typical of the Western world, since in the Third World it is cholera and hunger that are the severest scourges. But I believe that these are two closely intertwined vicious circles; for Indira Gandhi was right when she said that 'poverty is the worst pollution'.

1. Poverty leads to over-population, for when people are poor the only life insurance they have is the children who will look after them when they are old. But over-population leads to undernourishment, and not only to the consumption of the available foodstuffs, but to the exhaustion of the actual basis from which people live. That is the reason for the rapidly increasing destruction of nature in the countries of the Third World.

2. The world market is compelling the poorer countries to cut down their rain forests and to go over to monocultures for export, although these restrict and destroy their own subsistence economies. The world market is also forcing these countries to permit the location of industries which are environmentally dangerous (as in Bophal in India, for example) and to take over poisonous waste from the industrial nations (West Africa is one instance).

3. In countries with grave social injustices, there is nothing remarkable about ruthlessness towards nature. Violence towards weaker human beings justifies violence towards weaker nature. Where there is no social justice there will be no ecological justice either.

4. The terrible experience of the plague epidemics in fourteenth-century Europe was one reason why Europeans became so aggressive towards weaker nations and towards nature too. If people know that they are at the mercy of unfriendly natural forces and have no defence against them, they feel that they are engaged in an ongoing battle with nature.

5. Finally, turning to the spiritual dimension of faith in the cosmic Christ, let us remember the unknown saying of Jesus in the 77th Logion of the Gospel of Thomas:

> I am the light that is over them all.
> I am the All: the All has come forth from me
> and the All has returned to me.
> Cleave a piece of wood: I am there.
> Raise up a stone, and you will find me there.

Does this recognition not lead us to an expansion of the commandment: 'You shall love the Lord your God with all your heart and with all your soul and with all your strength, and this earth as yourself'? Let us sanctify life, for it is holy. Christ is within it.

VII

Jesus between Jews and Christians

I believe that for us men and women truth is to be found in dialogue. It is only in dialogue with one another that we can discover truth, because it is only in relationship to other people that we form our own identity. We always need the eyes of others if we are to understand ourselves and if we are to overcome our narcissism. When we encounter other people and hear them say 'I see you', 'I hear you' or 'I know you', we begin to see ourselves and understand ourselves. If it weren't for this experience of other people and their outside view of us, we should remain trapped in the prison of our own prejudgments and illusions about ourselves. No one loses his or her authentic identity in dialogue with other people. But in dialogue with other people everyone acquires a new profile.

For Jews, to enter into the dialogue between Jews and Christians (especially German Christians) is a very painful experience, for they do so in the presence of the victims of persecution, and the dead of Auschwitz. For Christians it is a humiliating experience too, full of pain, shame and ignominy, for to see ourselves reflected in the eyes of Jews means being looked at with the eyes of the dead and survivors of Auschwitz. And yet this is the only way to a perception of true history and our presence in it, and so it is the only way to an authentic Christian existence 'after Auschwitz'. Of course one doesn't invite one's victims to a dialogue. But the dialogue which Jews began with Christians in Germany after the Second World War is for us a costly gift. It is a prevenient offer, anticipating anything we could have expected, and it has given new hope to many of us who under the long shadows cast by Auschwitz had despaired.

In this dialogue we have come to recognize that from the very beginning our Christian tradition often formulated its beliefs about Christ – the central point of Christian theology – in an anti-Judaistic sense, and not in the pro-Judaistic way which would have been in accord with Jesus. Today, Jewish-Christian dialogue inspires us to formulate what we think about Christ afresh. It does not constrain us to give up our Christian identity, for then the Jews would have no partner in the dialogue. Nor does it constrain us to retract or reduce our belief in Jesus, the Christ of God, in order to make it conform to the Jewish faith in God; for then this Christian faith would cease to have any interest for Jews, and would have nothing more to say to them. But it does constrain us to see Jesus in a new way, and no longer just with our own eyes; we have to see him with the eyes of the Jews too, in dialogue.

1. The messianic perspective

There is no such thing as a christology or doctrine of Christ without any presuppositions; and its historical presupposition is the messianic promise of the Old Testament, and the Jewish hope which has its foundation in the Hebrew Bible. We can only truly and authentically understand Jesus if we perceive him and his history in the light of the Old Testament promises and present-day Judaism's history of hope. What does christology mean except messianology? 'The Christ' is Israel's messiah. Israel's messiah is 'Yahweh's anointed one', and to think of him means hoping for him and his redeeming sovereignty.

Of course Christian messianology takes its impress from the unique figure of Jesus, his message and his special history with God. But for all that, we must always have in mind the Old Testament and Israel's history, for it was in this that Jesus lived and it is this which gives him his theological significance as 'the Christ'. So here we shall not think of 'Christ' as a proper name (although the early Hellenistic congregations of course already did so). We shall see 'Christ' as the title for his function – his function for the men and women who are to be redeemed, and his function for the coming God. This means that we shall continually have to translate the name 'Christ' back into the title 'messiah', so that we can take in what it originally meant: Jesus is the messiah; the church is the messianic community; being a Christian means being human in the messianic sense. The name Christian is not the name for a party. It is a promise. It is what is messianic.

Here we shall be asking what the word 'messianic' meant for Judaism. What were the Jewish categories? From these we shall be able to develop the fundamental theological categories for the special christology of Jesus. Here the term messianic is intended to comprehend both the messiah as person, and the messianic kingdom, the messianic era and the messianic land, the messianic signs and the messianic people in history. Of course I am developing the concept 'messianic' in the light of Jesus' person and history. What else can a Gentile Christian do? But my purpose is to unfold the concept in so open a way that it respects the Jewish messianic hope, and is unfolded in continual dialogue with Jewish philosophers of religion. I am not presupposing that the Old Testament messianic hope points simply of itself to Jesus of Nazareth (which was what the theology of the prophetic proofs maintained). But I am

110

assuming that Jesus understood himself and his message in the expectation categories of this messianic hope, and that his followers saw him in these categories too, so that Jesus is linked with the messianic hope in a primal and indissoluble sense.

Christian beliefs about Christ have divided Christians and Jews. That is true. But this christology does not have to degenerate into a Christian anti-Jewish ideology, since hope for the messiah is also a bond between Christians and Jews, and this link is stronger than the division. Fellowship in contradiction is often stronger than fellowship in agreement. For that reason, no Christian christology must ever attempt to obliterate the Jewish hope for the messiah: Jesus is not 'the end of the messiah'. And for the same reason, no Christian christology must purpose to fall heir to the Jewish hope for the messiah, for, consciously or unconsciously, this means declaring that the testator is now dead: Jesus is not 'the fulfilment' of the messianic hope which puts an end to Israel. Finally, no Christian christology must ever surrender the hope for the messiah. Without it, Christianity will be paganized and will become anti-Jewish through indifference. Christian christology is a particular form of Israel's hope for the messiah, and it is still related to, and still dependent on, the Jewish forms of the messianic hope that came before Christianity and runs parallel to it.

'Messianism is Judaism's most profoundly original idea', claimed Martin Buber, rightly.[1] 'Messianism is the idea which Israel gave the world', maintained Gershom Scholem.[2] This is not just one Old Testament idea among others: the Old Testament as a whole is what von Rad called 'the book of a continually growing expectation', pointing beyond itself, and beyond every historical fulfilment. According to the prophetic interpretation, an explosive power builds up in Israel's history itself, and when 'the explosion comes, it is not revolutionary; it

111

is messianic'.[3] Christianity's mission has to be seen as the way in which Israel permeates the world of the Gentile nations with a messianic hope for the coming God. Christianity loses nothing by recognizing that its hope springs from this enduring Jewish root. Judaism surrenders nothing by recognizing what Martin Buber felt to be the 'mysterious' spread of the name, commandments and kingdom of its God by way of Christianity. This was the insight of the great Jewish philosopher Maimonides, in the Middles Ages, when he saw the phenomenon of Christianity as a *praeparatio messianica*, a messianic preparation of the nations for the universal coming of the kingdom of the God of Abraham. On the basis of this shared messianic hope, we shall try here to develop a christology in Christian-Jewish dialogue.

Messianic categories

Old Testament, Jewish and Christian messianism has such multifarious and equivocal manifestations that it is impossible to reduce them to any system. But because these manifestations are of central importance in the legacy of the Old Testament, it is useful to discover some of messianism's essential characteristics.

Gershom Scholem and Walter Benjamin pointed to the extraordinary experience of the historical breach out of which the messianic idea was born, and to which it itself again points. 'Jewish messianism is by origin and nature – and this cannot be too much stressed – a theory about a catastrophe,' wrote Scholem: 'This theory stresses the revolutionary, subversive element in the transition from every historical present to the messianic future.'[4] But here Scholem puts together two quite different revolutions: on the one hand the downfall; on the other the uprising. The first is a catastrophe, the second the deliverance. Both are leaps, as Scholem suggests: transition-less transitions. And the leap into the messianic future presupposes the downfall into the misery of the historical present. If we look back to the origin of Israel's messianic hope we can see that it was not simply born out of a historical disappointment (though this was Buber's psychological interpretation). It emerged quite specifically from the conquest of Israel by the Assyrian empire, the subjugation of the people, and their enslavement.

Gerhard von Rad emphatically stressed this theopolitical experience of the breakdown of the traditions and institutions by which Israel had up to then been sustained, and he therefore headed his volume on the 'Theology of Israel's Prophetic Traditions'[5] with the words of Isaiah 43.18f.: 'Remember not the former things nor consider the things of old. For behold, I purpose to do a new thing.' The break-off of the old is the precondition for the new, and what is prophetically new 'is – to use the controversial but unavoidable term – the eschatological' (p. 113). To be more precise, and using my own terminology: it is the messianic in the eschatological. The theological and political rupture of the old is a catastrophe. The catastrophe turns into 'the old' what has hitherto been the sustaining pillar, and so divides the times of history into a 'before' and an 'after' – divides them so radically that past and future can no longer appear on the same continuous temporal line. They have become two different eras or epochs. After the catastrophe, Israel in some sense arrived at zero point. It was threatened with self-dissolution, and in danger of paying homage to the victorious gods of those who had proved stronger. For its own catastrophe was at the same time the catastrophe suffered by its trust in God, and in this way it was even the catastrophe of its God himself. Is it possible still to be 'Israel' at all after a catastrophe like this? Apparently the people never felt that they were faced with this choice. Because God had chosen them, the choice was not open. The

113

consciousness of election must have been so strong that it preserved the people's identity.

This was 'the hour of the prophets', and the hour in which the messianic hope was born. The old traditions which had sunk and been forgotten in the cataclysm became remembrances pointing to the future, because of the hope for a new beginning – the new beginning which the electing God was going to give his people through his messiah.

Of course we can judge this as the idealization of a past time that can never be brought back. But before we make any such judgment, we should realize that this is a quite normal process of perception. It is only in exile that we first come to cherish the home country. It is only when we have been driven out of paradise that we know what paradise is. Every perception requires detachment and 'alienation'. That is why all self-knowledge is always a little too late, or a little too soon. The pressure of events blinds us to what these events are. So it is the messianic hope which makes clear for the first time what past history has to say about Yahweh's anointed, and about David. Hope for the new Jerusalem gives a present awareness of what the Jerusalem of old really was.

History understood as a continuous line, as development and progress, can only be the history of the victors, who wish to secure and expand their own power. History as it is experienced by the defeated, the subjugated and the enslaved is the experience of catastrophe and hope for deliverance; the experience of an enforced end and a longed-for new beginning; a downfall suffered and a new dawn hoped for. The catastrophe permits hope only for the overthrow of conditions as they have come to exist. This may be called the revolutionary element in the messianic hope.

Because of this, the question: when will the messiah come? does not receive a reply that has anything to do with time in its linear sense. It is answered through a determination of the

114

situation, the kairos or proper time which makes the messianic intervention possible and necessary. The conditions for the messiah's coming are named, but no date is given. 'The messiah will come when all his guests have sat down at table.' 'The messiah will come when the whole of Israel keeps a single sabbath – or when the whole of Israel keeps none.' This allows two possible conclusions:

1. The messiah will come when he is necessary. He will come when the need is greatest, and when people have given up hope. Because the messianic redemption is a response to the historical catastrophe, this catastrophe theory (which we have to call 'apocalyptic'), has a good deal in its favour. But of course it deprives the messiah of the liberty to come when he thinks best. It extorts his coming, so to speak, through its opposite: when the world plunges, and is plunged, into calamity, redemption will come out of what is most contrary to it. We come across this apocalyptic catastrophism again in our modern nuclear age. But its Armageddon theology is a miscalculation, and nothing other than a justification for the crime of the nuclear inferno.

2. The messiah will come when it is possible because the way has been prepared for him. This is the counsel of the prophets (Isa. 40). Prepare the way for the Lord! Repent! Arise, shine! Lift up your heads! The messiah doesn't come unheralded. He lets the gospel through which he announces himself go ahead of his coming. In this sense Buber may be right when he says that 'all time is immediate to redemption, all acts for God's sake may be termed messianic acts'.[6] This doesn't mean that good deeds bring the messianic redemption any closer; still less does it mean that good deeds are themselves the messianic redemption. But it does mean that hope for the coming of the messiah will already be messianically active here and now. That is what the Jewish Alenu prayer calls 'the betterment of the world for the kingdom of God'. The

115

Jews term this 'mending of the world' where a repair is needed a *tikun*. But of course the *tikun* is more than a 'repair' to the world, because the completion of all *tikun* is the kingdom of the messiah and, along the messiah's path, the kingdom of God itself. Since every *tikun* is the realization of some objective possibility, the splinters of the messianic era must already be exploded into the historical time of the present. In this sense every moment can be a messianic moment, 'every second can be the little door through which the messiah can enter'.[7] To prepare the way for the messiah means living in the light of Advent and, together with this world, becoming open for his coming. It means anticipating his coming in knowing and doing. It means 'now already' putting forth all our energies, in order, if we can, to let something become visible of the redemption of all things, which the messiah will perfect in his days.

Is this importunity? Does it mean 'pestering' the end to come, and 'compelling' the messiah to appear? It is certainly true that, as Scholem says, 'the allurement of action, the call to implement, to "bring it about"',[8] is inherent in the utopian elements of Jewish messianism. Christian messianism too is familiar enough with the upsurges of eschatological impatience for the implementation of what is hoped for. It was not merely the millenarian and revolutionary movements which were subject to this temptation – the Taborites, the Anabaptists and the Puritans. On the contrary, from Constantine onwards, the Christian empire itself and the clerical theocracy of the middle ages were viewed as the anticipatory vanguard of the promised eternal kingdom; and they perished on the rock of this idea. The difference between importuning the messiah by deepening the catastrophe, and importuning him by way of a high-handed establishment of his kingdom is not as great as Scholem thinks. The apocalyptists and the revolutionaries belong to the same family. Between them runs the line of a serenely unhurried passion for messianic action, an active hope, and the expectant liberation of the poor and oppressed – the line, that is, of the messianic *tikun* ethic.

Scholem movingly describes the great danger to which messianic thinking and living is subjected and calls it 'the price of messianism': 'There is a greatness about living in hope but it is also something profoundly unreal . . . The messianic idea in Judaism has enforced a deferred life, in which nothing can be done and accomplished in a final way.'[9]

The messianic hope can act in two opposite directions. It can draw the hearts of men and women away from the present into the future. Then it makes life in the present empty, and action in the present empty – and of course suffering over present oppression too. But it can also make the future of the messiah present, and fill that present with the consolation and happiness of the coming God. In this case what the messianic idea enforces is the very opposite of 'deferred life'. It is *life in anticipation*, in which everything must already be done and accomplished in a final way, because the kingdom of God in its messianic form is already 'at hand'.

What Scholem does not mention is the situation of the people who live with the messianic hope because with this hope they have survived the catastrophes. For the people who 'dwell in darkness' – the slaves, the prisoners, the exploited and oppressed – this hope is certainly not something unreal and remote. It is their only present reality. If they have self-respect and human dignity, then only in this hope and because of it. The messianic hope for a future which will change everything is the reason why prisoners do not come to terms with their prisons, and slaves do not submit to the slave-owners. Because of the messianic hope, they live 'with heads held high', in spite of the realities of the life they are living in the present. If it were not for this hope they would come to terms with this situation of slow death. They would bend

117

down to the dust until the dust no longer mattered. If they do not come to terms with the present, if they feel its injustice in pain, and rebel against it, then because of their unquenchable hope. 'A people only dies when its hope dies', says a Brazilian proverb, rightly.

3. Yet there is one unambivalent anticipation of the messianic era in the midst of the eras of history, and that is *the sabbath*. The weekly sabbath makes present the feast of creation in which God 'rested', and in which human beings and animals are to find rest too. Then 'Queen Sabbath' comes to the harassed and the exhausted, and raises them up. But in this way the sabbath also anticipates the messianic era. The songs at 'the third meal', on the afternoon of the sabbath, are 'heady with the intoxication of the messiah's certainly approaching future'.[10] In the present of the sabbath, the feast of creation, the feast of liberation and the feast of redemption are all celebrated at once. In terms of redemption, the sabbath can be called 'a sixtieth part of the coming world'.[11] Just as the sabbath represents a down payment on the messianic time, so the messianic time to come is conceived of as 'an endless sabbath'. We are told that 'when the whole of Israel keeps a single sabbath, the messiah will come'. That means that to keep the sabbath truly and together is the messianic time; and the reverse is also true. But it also means that in every true sabbath celebration the messiah enters the present through this little door, and together with Queen Sabbath comes among his people.

The weekly sabbath points beyond itself to the sabbath year, the sabbath year points beyond itself to the year of jubilee, the year of jubilee points towards the sabbath of the messianic era, and the sabbath of the messianic era points towards God's own eternal sabbath. The sabbath day is a kind of messianic intermezzo in the era of history, and the celebration of the sabbath is a kind of messianic 'sacrament of time'. Through the succession of sabbath days and sabbath years, 'the One who will come' moves time into the rhythms and vibrations of messianic expectation. The sabbath does not belong within the linear series of working days. It interrupts them, as human beings come to rest, and as nature too is allowed to rest. In this way the sabbath opens human beings and nature for the coming of the wholly-other time of the messiah. It makes them ready for the messiah's coming, in the midst of what is transitory.

Beside the noisy messianism of the apocalyptic of catastrophe, and the wild messianism of revolutionary utopianism, the sabbath is a still but steady, and thus lasting, messianism. It comes in everyday life, and brings the dream of redemption into the unnoticeable ordinariness of life as it is lived.

2. Jesus in Jewish-Christian dialogue

At the centre of all Jewish-Christian dialogue is the inexorable question about the messiah: 'Are you he who is to come, or shall we look for another?' Hope for the messiah leads us to Jesus, but it also hinders Jews from seeing Jesus as the expected messiah who has already come. Jesus replies to John the Baptist's messianic question through his proclamation, and his signs and wonders. The Gospels understand his whole coming and ministry in the contexts of Israel's messianic hope. And yet: it is the very same messianic hope which apparently makes it impossible for 'all Israel' to see Jesus as the messiah who has already come. Because earliest thinking about Jesus grew up in this field of tension, every Christian christology is forced to come back to this conflict, and has to struggle and come to terms with the Jewish 'no'. This is the fundamental question at the centre of Christian belief about Christ: Is the

Jewish 'no' anti-Christian? Is the Christian 'yes' anti-Jewish? Are the 'no' and the 'yes' final or provisional? Are they exclusive, or can they also take on a dialectically positive meaning for the people who feel compelled to utter them?

The Jewish no

Martin Buber formulated the Jewish objection to the messiahship of Jesus in his discussion with the New Testament scholar Karl-Ludwig Schmidt on January 14, 1933, in the Jewish seminary in Stuttgart, and he put it in such classic terms that his summing up has been continually echoed by other Jews ever since: 'The church rests on its faith that the Christ has come, and that this is the redemption which God has bestowed on mankind. We, Israel, *are not able* to believe this.' It is not a question of unwillingness, or hard-hearted defiance. It is an 'inability to accept'. Buber had a profound respect for Jesus, and even for Christianity; but his admission of this inability was impelled by a more profound experience still: 'We know more deeply, more truly, that world history has not been turned upside down to its very foundations – that the world is not yet redeemed. We *sense* its unredeemedness. The church can, or indeed must, understand this sense of ours as the awareness that *we* are not redeemed. But we know that that is not it. The redemption of the world is for us indivisibly one with the perfecting of creation, with the establishment of the unity which nothing more prevents, which is no longer controverted, and which is realized in all the protean variety of the world. Redemption is one with the kingdom of God in its fulfilment. An anticipation of any single part of the completed redemption of the world – for example the redemption beforehand of the soul – is something we cannot grasp, although even for us in our mortal hours redeeming and redemption are heralded. But we can perceive no caesura in history. We are aware of no centre in history – only its goal, the goal of the way taken by the God who does not linger on his way.'[12]

Schalom Ben-Chorin adopted this argument early on: 'The Jew is profoundly aware of this unredeemed character of the world, and he perceives and recognizes no enclave of redemption in the midst of its unredeemedness. The concept of the redeemed soul in the midst of an unredeemed world is alien to the Jew, profoundly alien, inaccessible from the primal ground of his existence. This is the innermost reason for Israel's rejection of Jesus, not a merely external, merely national conception of messianism. In Jewish eyes, redemption means redemption from all evil. Evil of body and soul, evil in creation and civilization. So when we say redemption, we mean the whole of redemption. Between creation and redemption we know only one caesura: the revelation of God's will.'[13] So according to Ben-Chorin there is after all one Jewish caesura in the history of this unredeemed world: the revelation of the Torah on Sinai, given to the people of Israel through Moses.

So can there be an anticipation or 'advance payment' of redemption in some part-sectors, before the final, total and universal redemption of the world? Can the Redeemer himself have come into the world before the redemption of the world has become a real happening? This is the central question of Christian existence: can one already be a Christian in this unredeemed world, which means existing as a messianic person?

But before we try to answer this critical challenge to Christian existence, we have to put the counter-question; for the argument about 'the unredeemed world' reflects on Jewish existence too. So as a Gentile Christian one must put this Gentile question to Israel: even *before* the world has been redeemed so as to become the direct and universal rule of God, can God already have a chosen people, chosen moreover for the very sake of this redemption? Doesn't Israel's election destroy Israel's solidarity with unredeemed humanity, even if the election is meant in a representative sense? And if this world is so totally unredeemed, isn't the Jewish caesura – the revelation on Sinai of God's will – an impossible possibility, in the midst of all this evil? And isn't it asking too much of Israel to expect her to obey that revealed will? To put the question in simpler and existential terms: can one already be a Jew in this godless world? After all the cruel persecutions by human beings, and in the abandonments by God, can one still be a Jew? But isn't Israel, the people of God's will and election, something quite unique in the world of the nations – something no one could ever have deduced? In the perspective of the messianic hope for the redemption of the world, we can be grateful for the miracle of Israel's prophetic existence. For if there were no advance radiance and no anticipation of redemption in this world, why should we think of the world as 'unredeemed' at all? The brutal fact of 'the unredeemed world' doesn't only speak against Christians. It speaks against Jews too. And it does so in both cases just because, and in so far as, Christians and Jews both, each in their own mode of existence, controvert the unredeemed world and resist its evils.

The Christian yes

This means that every enthusiastic claim that redemption has already been fulfilled must be banished from the christology of the church as it exists in the world of history. Jesus of Nazareth, the messiah who has come, is the suffering Servant of God, who heals through his wounds and is victorious through his sufferings. He is not yet the Christ of the parousia, who will come in the glory of God and redeem the world, so that it becomes the kingdom. He is the Lamb of God, not yet the Lion of Judah. What has already come into the world

122

through the Christ who has come and is present, is the justification of the godless and the reconciliation of enemies. What has not yet come is the redemption of the world, the overcoming of all enmity, the resurrection of the dead, and the new creation. Through Christ the love of God has become manifest. But the glory of God has not yet broken forth out of its hiddenness. That is why the life of Christians here and now is 'hid with Christ in God' by virtue of the hope that 'when Christ appears, then you also will appear with him in glory' (Col. 3.3–4). But just because through Christ men and women 'now already' have peace with God, they are 'no longer' prepared to come to terms with this peace-less world. Because they are reconciled with God, they suffer from this unredeemed world and 'sigh' with the whole enslaved creation (Rom. 8) for God's coming glory.

Even the raised Christ himself is 'not yet' the pantocrator. But he is already on the way to redeem the world. The Christian 'yes' to Jesus' messiahship is based on believed and experienced reconciliation; it will therefore accept the Jewish 'no', which is based on the experienced and suffered unredeemedness of the world. And the 'yes' will in so far make the 'no' its own as to talk about the total and universal redemption of the world only in the dimensions of a future hope and a present contradiction of this unredeemed world. So the Christian 'yes' to Jesus Christ is not in itself finished and complete. It is in itself open for Jesus' messianic future. It is an *anticipatory and provisional* 'yes', which looks to the end which God will bring about – 'Maranatha. Amen, come Lord Jesus' (Rev. 22.20).

This means that it cannot be an excluding and excommunicating 'yes', not even when it is uttered with the certainty of faith. Anyone who confesses Jesus as 'the Christ of God' is recognizing the Christ-in-his-becoming, the Christ on the way, the Christ in the movement of God's final, eschato-

123

logical history; and that person enters upon this way of Christ in the discipleship of Jesus. The earthly Jesus was on the way to the revelation of his messiahship. This is what people call Jesus' 'messianic secret'. The risen Lord is on the way to his sovereign rule, which is only beginning here, and is by no means universal; and his purpose is at the end to hand over the completed rule to God, who will then be 'all in all' (I Cor. 15.28) and will arrive at what Buber calls his 'direct theocracy'.

The earthly – the crucified – the raised – the present – the coming One: these are the stages of God's history with Jesus. It is these stages which the title 'Christ' gathers together, and it is these which should interpenetrate what we think and say about Christ and provide its framework. If we take this Christ-in-his-becoming, this Christ on the road, seriously, then we can take up a distinction that was made in the theology of an earlier time, and say that there can already be a *christologia viae* here and now, but there cannot yet be a *christologia patriae* – that is, there can be a christology of the way but not a christology of the home country. Until Christ's parousia, there can only be a historical christology, not yet a millenarian one. This shuts out every kind of ecclesiastical and political triumphalism, for the christology of the way is a theology of the cross and nothing else. The coming One is in the process of his coming and can be understood only in that light: as on the road, and walking with us. But for that very reason every confession of Christ in the history of this unredeemed world has to be understood as a reaching out, an anticipation of the new creation in which every tongue will confess him in the glory of the Father (Phil. 2.11). Every confession of Christ leads to the way, and along the way. It is not yet itself the goal.

Jesus the Lord as the early community of Christians acknowledged him is on the way to his rule, not merely through the coming times, but through present spaces as well. He takes the road from Jerusalem to the ends of the earth (Acts

1.8), from Israel to the Gentiles, from the Gentiles to Israel again, and back to Jerusalem (Rom. 11.26). He takes the road from the church to the poor, and from the poor to the kingdom of God. The way of Christ comes into being under the feet of the person who walks it. To tread the way of Christ means believing in him. Believing in him means accompanying him along the part of the road he is taking at the present moment. 'I am the way', says Jesus about himself according to one of the old Johannine sayings (John 14.6).

God's yes in the Jewish no

If the Jewish 'no' to Jesus' messiahship is due to 'inability', as Buber said, and not to unwillingness or ill-will, then there is no reason for Christians to deplore this 'no' or to make it a reproach. Israel's 'no' is not the same as the 'no' of unbelievers, which can be found everywhere. It is a special 'no' and must be respected as such. In his Israel chapters, Romans 9 to 11, Paul saw God's will in Israel's 'no'. It is not because it says 'no' that Israel's heart has been hardened. It is because God hardened its heart that it cannot do anything but say 'no'. Hardness of heart is not the same thing as rejection, and has nothing whatsoever to do with a moral judgment. To harden the heart is a historically provisional act on God's part, not an eschatologically final one. It is an act performed for a particular purpose, as the story of Moses and Pharaoh shows.

But we then have to ask: what is the purpose? Why does God impose on the whole of Israel an 'inability' to say the 'yes' of faith to Jesus? The answer is: so that the gospel might pass from Israel to the Gentiles, and 'the last' be first. 'Blindness has come upon part of Israel, until the full number of the Gentiles come in' (Rom. 11.25). Without Israel's 'no', the Christian church would have remained an inner-Jewish messianic revival movement. But because of the Jewish 'no', the Christian community had a surprising experience. It discovered that the Spirit of God comes upon Gentiles so that they are seized by faith in Christ directly, without becoming Jews first of all. The mission to the Gentiles which Paul himself began is an indirect fruit of the Jewish 'no'. Paul emphasizes this to the Christian congregation in Rome, to which both Jews and Christians belonged: 'As regards the gospel they are enemies of God for your sake; but as regards election they are beloved for the sake of their forefathers' (11.28). It is therefore perfectly correct to say that 'We shall only put antisemitism behind us when we succeed theologically in making something positive out of the Jewish "no" to Jesus Christ'.[14] The 'something positive' is the mission to the Gentiles out of which the church emerged. It is not just a matter of plucking something positive out of something negative – 'making the best' of something that is in itself bad. According to Paul, it is God's will which is manifested in the Jewish inability to accept the gospel of Christ. That is why Paul, the Jewish Christian, can certainly deplore the Jewish 'no', and grieve for his own people (9.2–5), but at the same time he can also praise the divine 'yes' which manifests itself out of this 'no': 'Their failure means riches for the world' (11.12), 'their rejection is the world's reconciliation' (11.15).

There can be no question of God's having finally rejected the people of his choice – that would mean that he rejected his own election (11.29) – and of his then having sought out another people instead, i.e., the church. Israel's promises remain Israel's promises. They have not been transferred to the church. Nor has the church supplanted Israel from its place in the divine history. In the perspective of the gospel, Israel has by no means become 'like all the nations'. Finally, Israel's 'no' does not make it a witness in history to God's judgment, so that it now exists merely as a warning to the community of

Christ not to fall away from faith. Just because the gospel has come to the Gentiles as a consequence of the Jewish 'no', it will return – indeed it must return – to Israel. 'The first shall be last.' Israel is 'the last' towards which everything draws.

For Paul this was an apocalyptic 'mystery': 'Blindness has come upon a part of Israel, until the full number of the Gentiles come in, and so all Israel will be saved; as it is written, "The Deliverer will come from Zion, he will banish ungodliness from Jacob"' (11.25–26). For Paul, Israel's 'Deliverer' is the Christ of the parousia, the messiah who will come in the glory of God and whose name is Jesus. The Jewish 'no', which as Saul he maintained so zealously against the early Christian congregations, was overthrown through a call vision of the crucified and glorified Jesus. That is why Paul puts his hope for his people in the Deliverer 'from Zion', who is going to come in visible glory. He does not expect that this Deliverer will bring about the Jews' conversion, and that they will arrive at Christian faith. What he expects is Israel's redemption, and that she will be raised from the dead: 'What will their acceptance mean but life from the dead?' (11.15). Israel will be delivered because she sees glory; and this will not happen merely to the final generation. Cutting right through the times of history, it will happen to all the dead at once, 'in a moment'. The apostle's hope of redemption therefore embraces all Israel at all times. His practical answer to the Jewish 'no' is not anti-Judaism but the evangelization of the nations. For him, this brings the day of her redemption closer for Israel too.

The same Christ Jesus is not the same for everyone, because people are different. He has one profile for the poor and another for the rich, one profile for the sick and another for the healthy. So the same Christ Jesus has one particular profile for Jews and another for Gentiles: 'For I tell you that Christ became a servant to the Jews to show God's truthfulness, in

127

order to confirm the promises given to the patriarchs, and in order that the Gentiles might glorify God for his mercy . . .' (Rom. 15.8–9a). According to this, Jesus is Israel's messiah, the one who finally endorses and fulfils the promises given to her; and he is at the same time the one who has mercy on the Gentiles and is their saviour, the saviour who brings them to the praise of God. And in each case he is the one for the sake of the others:

As Israel's messiah he becomes the saviour of the Gentiles. In Jesus, Israel herself encounters the Gentiles – Israel with her whole history, in a nutshell and in messianic form. That is why Matthew tells the story of Jesus, not as an individual history, but as Israel's collective biography, from the flight into Egypt, the call out of Egypt, the days of temptation in the wilderness, down to the story of the passion. Israel's messiah is at the same time Israel's representative. In Jesus Christ, Israel herself encounters believers from the nations in messianic form. Because Christ opens Israel to the Gentiles, the Gentiles for their part are gathered into the divine history of promise and faithfulness towards Israel.

On the other hand, Jesus encounters Israel as the saviour of the nations, believed in and adored by many from all peoples. In this form – not directly, that is, but indirectly – he manifests himself to Israel as her messiah. In the risen Lord of the church of the nations, the peoples look towards Israel and remind Israel of the promise to Abraham and of Abraham's faith. The only justifiable Gentile Christian 'mission to the Jews' is the reminder to the Jews of their own gracious election, and its promise for humanity. This is surely what Paul means by 'making Israel jealous' for the faith that saves (Rom. 11.14). The faith that is meant is the faith whose 'father' is Abraham (Rom. 4.16), and which Paul proclaims as the justifying, saving faith in Christ. In the name of Abraham's faith, Christians and Jews can already become one here and now;

for, just like Jewish faith, Christian faith desires to be nothing other than the faith of Abraham.

If, then, the Christian 'yes' has to be looked for in this direction – if it is the 'yes' which discovers in the Jewish 'no' what is positive, and God's will – then this must also be the approach taken by a 'Christian theology of Judaism' in a doctrine of Christ that is pro-Judaistic, not anti-Judaistic. But this is possible for Christian theology only if Jewish theology tries on the basis of the Jewish 'no' to understand what Buber calls 'the mystery' of Christianity. After Auschwitz, that is certainly asking a very great deal. But for believing Jews too it might nevertheless perhaps be a theological question: what divine will is really expressed in the mission and spread of Christianity? For since the name of the Lord has been made known to the ends of the earth through the mission of the gospel, Christians throughout the world pray daily with Israel for the hallowing of God's name, the doing of his will, and the coming of his kingdom. Cannot Israel, in spite of its own observance of the Jewish 'no', view Christianity as 'the messianic preparation' of the nations, and so see in it the way which its own hope for the messiah takes to the nations?

VIII

'Behold I Make All Things New': The Great Invitation

If we want to know about our future as human beings we read the newspapers. If we want to know more about it still, we read the Annual Reports of the Worldwatch Institute. Our political leaders study what their secret services have to say. But what do these things tell us about the future of the world? All we really know about it is that we don't know, and that things will probably turn out differently from what we think. Who knew anything about the changes in eastern Europe before they took place in 1989? The future is unforeseeable. Who reckoned with the collapse of Communism in 1991?

So if we want to know God's future, where can we look? We cannot find it in the stars, as the astrologers believe. We cannot read it from the Tarot cards, as the fortune-tellers maintain. Simplistic though it sounds: we find this future in the Bible. This 'good old book' is the book of God's promises. It tells how men and women have experienced God's faithfulness to these promises. The Bible is the book of remembered hopes, for it is the book of God's future: God's future in the past, God's future in the present, God's future in times to come.

If we ask the man or woman in the street in Moscow or

Washington, Tokyo, London, or wherever we happen to live, how they see the future, what are we likely to hear? They will talk about their existential fears, their concern about the nature we have polluted and the environment we have destroyed and, not least, the nuclear armaments which are escaping our control. We are again living in an age of anxiety, and our anxieties are justified, because they warn us about the dangers of the future. But there are also an increasing number of people who feel completely superfluous, and who in fact *are* superfluous, if we look at the matter objectively. These 'surplus people' have a brutally frank answer to our question. They say: for us there is no future. This is the 'no future' generation.

If we could ask the people in the Bible how they see the future, what should we hear? Abraham and Sarah would tell us about God's promise, which turned them into asylum-seekers in alien lands. Moses and Miriam would talk about the God of the Exodus, and the vision of the promised land of liberty. Isaiah and Jeremiah would speak about the messiah and the new covenant. John the Baptist and Mary, Peter and Martha would tell about Jesus, and about the kingdom of God which has come so close to us in him. From the beginning to the end, the people of the Bible are people of hope. All of them saw the star of promise in the long night of this world, and glimpsed the first streaks of the daybreak colours heralding God's new day. They all set out to look for this future of God's, for they all heard the invitation: 'come, for all is now ready.'

Today, we ourselves belong to both groups of people. We read the newspapers, and are filled with anxiety. We read the Bible, and hope for God. Like everyone else, we are afraid of the dangers ahead of us in this world. Like the people in the Bible, we believe that God's deliverance is near. This is an age of anxiety. That is true. But it is an age of hope too. We believe in God and hope for his coming, but we are not optimists – we are afraid for our world. We are afraid of the things that imperil

131

its future: we can imagine the social catastrophes in Russia – we can calculate the ecological disaster in our own countries – we know more than we can believe. But we are not pessimists, for we have faith in God and believe that he will never let his creation go. People who hope for God are not optimists. They don't need the power of positive thinking. People who hope for God are not pessimists. They don't need the logic of negative dialectic. People who trust in God know that God is waiting for them, that God is hoping for them, that they are invited to God's future, so that they are holding in their hands the most marvellous invitation they have ever had in their lives.

I should like first to look at the biblical texts, in order to see what the new thing is that has come about from God's side. Then I should like to work forward to a theological judgment, and to open the theological discussion about God's future by putting five questions and suggesting five answers. Finally, I should like to know how we can 'evangelize' today, and that means: how can we help men and women and our world to open themselves for God's future? For the invitation to the new creation of all things has to be different from the missions of the self-propagating ecclesiastical Christianity we have known hitherto.

1. God comes to the world to renew it: biblical perspectives

The first perspective is *the great vision of God's future* in the book of Revelation: '. . . and God will wipe away every tear from their eyes, and death shall be no more, neither shall there be mourning nor crying nor pain any more, for the former things have passed away. And he who sat upon the throne said, "Behold, I make all things new"' (Rev. 21.1–5a).

John, who had been banished to the island of Patmos because of his faith, 'saw' this new creation of all things (1.2). Where did he see it? He says: 'I was in the Spirit on the Lord's day' (1.10). What he saw there overwhelmed him, just as it overwhelmed the apostles at Easter and Paul at his call. He saw the humiliated and crucified Christ in the radiance of God's glory, and on this resurrection day of Christ's he saw 'the Last Judgment', the end of the old world in the dawn of the world that God makes new. The end of the world is not night, nuclear winter, the darkness of hell, the eternal shadow-world of death. The end of the world is the new day of eternal life. Like the first creation, the new creation of all things begins with the light which dispels the darkness, the light which a German hymn describes as the 'morning radiance of eternity'. It is not the absolute eternity of God. It is the new time of the new creation, the eternal springtime of the life in which what has been withered and dried up blossoms, and what has been dead comes alive again. 'Behold, I make all things new.' That is a creation which endures and never passes away, a beginning without an end.

Whom does John see? He sees the infinite, eternal God coming to the finite beings he has created and to this vulnerable earth. God comes to his transitory creatures on this earth to live among them, and now finally to find rest in his creation as he once did on the sabbath. God will not seek out his dwelling place in special temples or cathedrals. He wants to make his whole creation his home: 'Heaven is my throne and the earth is my footstool' (Isa. 66.1; Acts 7.49). The cosmos is his temple; chaos is his enemy. That is why the beauty of the new creation will drive out chaos. Heaven and earth are waiting to become God's house, for everything created has been made for love. God's Spirit is in them all and throws them open for God's future. God finds no rest until everything he has created has returned home to him, like the prodigal son in the parable.

133

This means that God is still restless in history until the world becomes his sanctuary and he can enter into all created things and find a home there. New creation means: 'He will dwell with them, and they shall be his people.' The creator is not far off from his creation any more, standing outside it in remote detachment. He moves into his creation, to live there. And then his own eternal livingness becomes the energy which makes those he has created live, and lets the human beings he has made, find in his presence room to live, room to expand and develop, and room to love. His eternal light irradiates creation and warms every living thing, filling them all with divine energies. His eternal presence unites what death has separated. Once this happens, death, darkness, cold and chaos disappear from creation. When the living God comes as close to us as this, the dead will live and death will be no more. When his glory is revealed, his beauty will redeem the world, as Dostoievsky said. When God comes as close to us as this, the remoteness from God which we feel as we weep over graves disappears. God finds a home among human beings, and human beings find a home with God. People and animals, earthly and heavenly beings will become neighbours and fellow householders in the house of God they share. This is what John saw on Patmos: the future of this weary and heavy-laden world in God, and God's future in the new, liberated and happy world.

The second perspective is the experience of God's coming among us *in Christ*. 'God was in Christ reconciling the world to himself . . . If anyone is in Christ, he is a new creation; the old has passed away; behold, everything has become new' (II Cor. 5.19, 17). What happens for us and in us through Christ has two sides to it: in Christ we find God, and we find ourselves in Christ.

This is the true God: the one who in Christ takes the way of suffering to the point of death on the cross, so as to reconcile this faithless and torn world to himself; the one who takes on himself death in profoundest forsakenness so as to comfort all the forsaken through his love; the one who becomes poor so as to make the poor rich. In Christ God himself comes to us and reconciles us with himself. And that is our true self: our sins, which cut us off from the source, the wellspring of life, are forgiven. Our enmity is overcome. God reconciles us, and we are reconciled. God loves us, and we are beloved.

If we live in Christ then we have this unique experience of God. God has arrived with us. He is so present, so close, that in him we live and move and have our being. If we live in Christ then we have this unique experience of the self: we have arrived at God. We are good, just and beautiful, like a newly made creature on the first day of creation. The 'old things' are the burden of injustice and violence that weighs us down; and now this can be thrown away like an old coat. The new thing which is the springtime of the whole creation has already taken hold of us.

With the reconciliation which we experience, our transformation begins. Through this reconciliation, what is going to be God's future, according to the great vision in Revelation 21, already arrives among us here and now. Where the divine reconciliation takes hold of us, the tears are already wiped away, and suffering and crying already end, for 'the former things' – the old nature – has passed away. Paul 'sees' the same thing as John on Patmos. He too challenges us to open our eyes and to see our life in Christ: 'See, everything has become new.' This is not a mystical faith with closed eyes. It is a messianic faith with eyes wide open. He even adds 'everything has become new.' This can surely only mean that anyone who sees themselves and the world with the eyes of Christ sees them as 'reconciled', in spite of their enmity and tornness – sees them, that is, as a world that has already been newly created. Even the people who oppose us are no longer our deadly enemies. They are men and women for whom Christ died and whom God has already reconciled with himself, whether they know it or not. How can we take our own atheism and the atheism of our fellow human beings more seriously than the real reconciliation of the true God with us all?

The third perspective is the experience of *God's presence* in us in *the Spirit of life*. 'Truly I say to you, unless one is born anew he cannot see the kingdom of God' (John 3.3). What Paul calls the new creation in Christ, John calls the new birth from God's Spirit. What according to Paul has happened in Christ for us without our doing – reconciliation – is according to John efficacious or active in us through the rebirth of our life from the Spirit. The two metaphors are complementary: God makes new people of us through the work of reconciliation, and out of the Spirit of God we are reborn as if from a mother. So we are new creations of the Father and children of the Holy Spirit. The being-in-Christ and the new life-from-the-Spirit are two sides of the same thing, but they express something different. What are we describing when we use the metaphor about rebirth? We are describing the experience of an overflowing, exuberant joy in living. People who experience the Holy Spirit experience God's vital energy. They feel new-born. They are flooded with light. They are interpenetrated by love. Their abilities are charged with new energies. The rebirth of life from acts of violence and guilt, from the faults and hurts of everyday life and, finally, from the shadows of death is a tremendous affirmation of life. It brings new vitality into body and soul and is not an unworldly spirituality. If we replace the world 'Spirit' by the Hebrew word *ruach*, tempest, we see at once what experiences of the self go hand in hand with the experience of this divine force.

Life begins at every moment when we are moved by the Spirit. Through rebirth from the Holy Spirit our transitory life becomes eternal life. For what is born of God is eternal and never passes away. Eternal life is not something that just begins after death. It begins here and now in the rebirth from the eternal Spirit we experience. There is eternal life before death. We do not experience it in terms of its length, as a life without end. We experience in terms of its depth. Every truly and wholly lived moment is the presence of eternity, and is imperishable. With the experience of the Spirit, the springtime of life begins, whether we are young or old. The well of life, as the Holy Spirit has been called from earliest times, springs up in us once more (John 4.14). We become fruitful again, as trees, young and old, do in the spring. The rebirth of the whole cosmos (Matt. 19.28) begins in us. The eschatological springtime of the whole creation stirs us into life. In the Spirit, the new creation of all things begins, with us.

The fourth perspective is *God's challenge* to a new *way of living*: 'But be renewed in the spirit of your minds, and put on the new nature, created after the likeness of God in true righteousness and holiness' (Eph. 4.23f.). This new life acquires its contours in the discipleship of Christ, and its inner strength from the life-giving Spirit. According to the witness of people in the Bible, it means breaking with the pattern of this world which is so profoundly out of joint, not 'being conformed to this world' (Rom. 12.2), but anticipating the divine new creation of all things, and the rebirth of life. For Paul that meant a change from darkness to light: 'The night is far gone, the day is at hand. Let us then cast off the works of darkness and put on the armour of light . . .' (Rom. 13.12). It is like a change from being asleep to being awake. What he meant by this was not just a new personal morality. He meant a wholly new life in righteousness and holiness, personally and in community with other people, in community with other

137

people and politically, politically and ecologically, with all the energies of the Spirit in us, and in all the possibilities which God opens up for us.

As long ago as 1968 the General Assembly of the World Council of Churches in Uppsala took as its motto: 'Behold, I make all things new.' Its message was an excellent formulation of God's challenge to the renewal of life: 'We ask you, trusting in God's renewing power, to join in this anticipation of God's kingdom, showing now something of the newness which Christ will complete on his day.'

In these four biblical perspectives we see God coming to us in one single movement. This movement begins with what comes last – the great vision of God's future: 'Behold, I make all things new' – then it advances to the special coming of God among us in faith in Christ: 'In Christ a new creation' – to his presence in the experience of the Spirit: 'Born anew from the Holy Spirit' – and to his challenge to us: 'play your part in the new creation of all things!' But that means: God's future has already begun. The new creation of all things is already underway. We are invited to be part of it.

2. God's future and his righteousness: some theological questions and answers

With the help of these biblical insights, let us try to answer some of the theological questions which are often asked in connection with 'God's future'.

What can we know about God's future, and how can we talk about it?

There are two ways of talking about the future. One is the method called *extrapolation*. The other is the method of *anticipation*. All researchers into the future and all planners for the future extrapolate, inferring the future from the data and trends of the past and the present. By means of trend analyses, computer forecasts and probability assessments they enquire into what is going to be. For them, the past and the future lie along one and the same straight, temporal line. There is no *qualitative* difference between past and future. So they are not really investigating the future at all. They are simply prolonging into the future their own present. What they understand by future is the extrapolated and extended present, and by way of this understanding they repress the future's new possibilities. According to this interpretation of things, the future is what is going to *be*, not what is going to *come*. There is only the eternal becoming-and-passing-away. There is no final Advent.

The method of anticipation works quite differently. Anticipation means expectation and an advance realization of what is coming. In our anxiety we apprehend and anticipate coming danger. In our hope we apprehend and anticipate coming happiness. But it is not merely these feelings of the heart which anticipate the awareness of what is ahead. Our ideas and concepts do so too. Anticipations are advance pictures and pre-conceptions (in the literal sense) of what we are looking for and expect. They are creative imaginations of what is to come. Without these search-images in our understanding minds, our senses would discover nothing. But once we find what we are looking for, our experiences always correct our expectations. Consequently the anticipation of what is going to come always involves the preparedness for surprise. For the method of anticipation, there is a qualitative difference between past and future. It is the simple difference between reality and potentiality. The past is the reality, the future is the possible, and the present is the front at which potentialities can be realized or thwarted. I can tell about the past, because it

139

lies there, finished and done with. But I can grasp the future only through the method of anticipation; for the person who tells the future turns it into the past. In this interpretation, the future is not what *will be*; it is what is coming to meet us. English makes this point when it talks about 'the coming year'. This is the advent-like understanding of future.

If we then apply these distinctions to our question, we arrive at the following answers:

– Talk about God's future is not a commentary on future history. It is a promise of the future of all human history.

– Talk about God's future is not an extrapolation from the past and the present. It is an anticipation of God's new world in the midst of this old one.

– God's future is experienced only in expectation of its coming. The new creation in Christ which we experience, and the rebirth from the Spirit which we experience, are the true anticipations of God's future which makes all things new.

What happens to the apocalyptic of the end of the world in the hope for God's future?

In the Christian doctrine about 'the Last Things' we talk about God's future in two ways: it is the completion or consummation of history, and it is the end of history. Just because it is the consummation of creation and God's history of promise, it is also the end of this corrupted world-time of sin and death, injustice and violence. Revelation 21 says : 'Behold I make all things new.' But before that promise we are told: 'the former things have passed away' (see too II Cor. 5.17). Apocalyptically we look at the downfall of this world; eschatologically we look at the resurrection of the world God will make new. So the two belong together. If we were to look only at the goal – 'Behold, I make all things new' – we should become optimists, shutting our eyes to the pain and the tears.

140

If we were to look only at the end we should become pessimists, despising or discounting God's grace which is new every morning. End-of-the-world apocalyptic is just as un-Christian as a naive faith in progress. In fact it is only the reverse side of the same coin. A Christian theology of history does not teach that everything is going to get better and better. Nor does it say that everything is going to get worse and worse. What it does tell us is that with the coming deliverance the danger grows too. The evil grows together with the good, and where Christ is present the Antichrist is found as well. When men and women are in accord with God in their lives, other people's opposition to God increases. The conflicts spread and become more violent. Things become more and more critical in the world. History itself is nothing other than permanent crisis. That is why so many people dream about 'the end of history' – most recently Francis Fukuyama of the State Department in Washington, who sees the end of history dawning in the victory of the liberal Democrats and the global marketing of everything. But every anticipated end of history only takes history further and makes it more critical and more dangerous still. We can sum up this paradox of history in two sentences:

'Where there is danger, deliverance grows too.' Those are the consoling words of the German poet Friedrich Hölderlin.

'Where deliverance is near, danger grows.' That was the threatening response of the German philosopher Ernst Bloch.

Both statements are correct. That is why fear of danger is part of trust in deliverance, and the apocalyptic dread of the world's annihilation belongs to hope for its new creation.

Does God's future just mean new creation? Does it not bring judgment too?

Judgment on the old existence is the precondition for the

creation of the new. Without the 'last judgment' there is no new creation. But what *is* God's judgment, and what is its purpose? According to biblical idea, through the divine judgment God's righteousness and justice will be made to prevail over wrong and injustice everywhere. For only God's justice creates peace. In his judgment, God becomes the one who judges the nations in peace (Pss. 94, 96–99). The messiah king will 'establish and uphold [Israel] with justice and with righteousness' (Isa. 9.7). He will 'judge the poor with righteousness and decide with equity for the meek of the earth' (Isa. 11.4). God's judgment has nothing to do with vengeance or retribution. It has to do with the victory of God's creative and saving righteousness and justice. Before 'the judgment seat of Christ' too it is not a question of retribution for our sins, but of the justice of God which creates justice, puts things to rights, and justifies. The purpose of judgment is not condemnation. Its purpose is the resocialization of the sinner in the kingdom of God.

God's judgment in the Last Judgment is not God's last word. His last word is: 'Behold, I make all things new.' The Last Judgment is in fact provisional. The final thing is the new creation. Judgment ministers to the new creation. So there is no need for us to be afraid of it. We can hope for it. It is high time that we stopped threatening people with God's judgment and infusing them with the fear of judgment. The message of God's Last Judgment is good news, a liberating message – the message that justice exists, and that there is one who finally guarantees it. So the murderers will not eternally triumph over their victims.

Does the new creation of all things mean 'universal reconciliation' and 'the restoration of all things'?

This is a difficult question, because only God will answer it.

142

If we think humanistically and universally – God could perhaps be a particularist. But if we think pietistically and particularistically – God might be a universalist. If I examine myself seriously, I find that I have to say: I myself am not a universalist, but God may be one. One can also find a subtle way out of the question, as Karl Barth did when he said: 'I don't teach universal reconciliation but I don't not-teach it.' I will neither evade the question in the one way or the other, but will reply to it with a confession of hope which I learnt from Christoph Blumhardt: 'The confession of hope has completely slipped through the church's fingers . . . There can be no question of God's giving up anything or anyone in the whole world, either today or in eternity . . . The end has to be: Behold, everything is God's! Jesus comes as the one who has borne the sins of the world. Jesus can judge but not condemn. My desire is to have preached this to the lowest circles of hell, and I will never be confounded.'[1]

Let me take this up and say: I am not preaching universal reconciliation. I am preaching the reconciliation of all men and women in the cross of Christ. I am not proclaiming that everyone will be redeemed, but it is my trust that the proclamation will go forward until everyone has been redeemed. Universalism is not the substance of the Christian proclamation; it is its presupposition and its goal. 'Behold, I make all things new': if that really is God's future, then everyone is invited and no one is shut out. Even for the people who reject it, the invitation stands, for it is God's invitation.

Is there a hell?

Yes, I believe there is a hell. In the horrors of Auschwitz and in the terrors of Vietnam, people experienced a hell of suffering and a hell of guilt. That is why we talk about the hell of Auschwitz and the hell of Vietnam, meaning a senseless

143

suffering with no way out, an unforgivable guilt and a fathomless abandonment by God and human beings. Is there a hell after death too? I believe there is, for the hell before death is worse than death itself. For many people death was a release from the suffering and fear of that hell.

Do we know anyone who is in hell? Would we tell a mother weeping at her son's grave that her son is in hell because he never found faith while he was alive? We should respond to the first question with an embarrassed silence. And we would not answer 'yes' to the second one either. But I know someone who was in hell: it is Jesus Christ, who the creed says 'descended into hell'.

When we were thinking about the tortured Christ, we asked: what does this article in the creed mean? When did Christ go through hell? And we saw that in the past two answers have been given. The earlier interpretation said that after his death Christ descended to the realm of the dead, to preach to them the gospel of their redemption and to deliver them. Luther looked at it differently, maintaining that Christ endured the torments of hell between Gethsemane and Golgotha, in his profound forsakenness by God. But whatever we may think about Christ's descent into hell, Luther was right when he said: 'Regard not hell and the eternity of torment in thyself, nor these things in themselves, nor yet in those who are damned. Look upon the face of Christ, who for thy sake descended into hell and was forsaken by God as one who is damned eternally, as he said on the cross: "My God, why hast thou forsaken me?" See, in him thy hell is vanquished . . .'[2] Because Christ was in hell and endured its torments, there is hope in hell for redemption. Because Christ was raised to life from hell, hell's gates are open and its walls have been broken down. 'Though I make my bed in hell, you are there.' And then hell is not hell any longer. 'O hell where is thy victory? But thanks be to God, who gives

144

us the victory through our Lord Jesus Christ? (I Cor. 15.55, 57).

3. The gospel of God's future

What has the gospel got to do with the future? Jesus brings
God's future to us human beings, and we are invited to God's
future. This is a new angle on things, and it requires a new
kind of practical application. Up to now we have known
evangelization only as the spread of the present into the
future, not as an actual anticipation of the future itself. Up to
now, the purpose of evangelization was either to extend
Christian civilization, or to propagate the church, or to spread
one's own experience of faith. This was not mission in the
perspective of the end – not the mission of God's kingdom –
not an invitation to God's future. That is why Christian
missions have done more to bring Christian denominational-
ism into the world than to prepare the way for God's kingdom.
But what are we really aiming to do when we witness to the
gospel, and proclaim it?

1. In substance, we come across the word 'gospel' for the
first time in the book of Isaiah (52.7), where it means the joyful
message that heralds the liberating sovereignty of God. It
means the messengers who announce God's coming to the
people, and by announcing it put God's new era into effect. In
the New Testament too the gospel is a messianic force: it is the
kingdom of God in the form of the Word. It is the provisional
parousia of Christ. 'Where the gospel is proclaimed, the
exalted Lord in his word on human lips hastens ahead of his
appearance; there he anticipates his future in the announcement of himself as the Coming One', writes the New Testament scholar Heinrich Schlier.[3] So in the New Testament,
gospel and evangelization are messianic concepts. They are
the word and the language through which God reveals his

145

future and makes his new creation of all things known. So the gospel is also the word which liberates the captives and justifies the sinners, which wipes away the tears and raises up men and women who are burdened and bowed down. The gospel is the announcement of the messianic era: 'The night is far gone, God's day is near!' The gospel is the invitation to God's future. People who believe the gospel experience the powers of the future world (Heb. 6.5). They move into the springtime of the new creation.

2. Evangelization is *an invitation*, nothing more than that and nothing less. It is not instruction, and not an attempt at conversion either. It is a plea: 'Be reconciled with God!' The people who consciously or unconsciously witness to the gospel, and the people who are commissioned to proclaim it, have no authority except the authority of this plea. It is the authority of the pleading Christ, who carries our sins on the cross and with his outstretched arms invites us: 'Come, for all is now ready'. The pleading Christ doesn't force us, and he doesn't threaten 'unless you decide today you'll go to hell'. The pleading Christ begs for his invitation to be accepted. He appeals to the people invited, but the appeal is based on their freedom. In Christ, God has reconciled the world with himself, so be reconciled with God! Reconciliation is possible. So here too we are told: God is going to create everything anew, so seize these opportunities. They are there already, in yourself and close to yourself. Peace is possible. Justice is possible. Liberation is possible. God has made the impossible possible, and we are invited to seize our possibilities for living. Participate in the renewal of society and nature!

3. How does this invitation to God's future differ from mission through the dissemination of Christianity as it now is? To put it simply: it differs through its hope for what is new. We don't want to spread Western civilization. We want to invite people in all civilizations to the new creation of all things. We

don't want to expand the sphere of influence of the church 'outside which there is no salvation'. We want to experience the new creations of God's Spirit in other cultures. We shouldn't try to turn everyone into Lutherans or Baptists, or found Roman Catholic congregations everywhere. But wherever we proclaim God's kingdom, God's people gather together, just of themselves, and will have their own experiences and develop their own forms of belief and worship. The new creation is as rainbow-hued and diversified as creation at the beginning. Ecclesiastical uniformity suppresses the pluralism of the Holy Spirit and its charismata.

The kingdom of God isn't there for the sake of the church. The church is there for the sake of the kingdom. So – as we said at the very beginning – all the church's own concerns and interests must be subordinated to Jesus' concern for God's kingdom. The church's concern is not the church. It is more than that. The church has to do with God and his future for all men and women. It has to do with the new creation of all things for eternal life.

Notes

II *The Passion of Christ and the Pain of God*

1. E. Wiesel, 'Der Mitleidende Gott' in R. Walter (ed.), *Die hundert Namen Gottes*, Freiburg 1985, 70.
2. J. Sobrino, preface to O. A. Romero, *Die Notwendige Revolution*, Mainz and Munich 1982.
3. D. Bonhoeffer, *Letters and Papers from Prison*, ed. E. Bethge, trans. R. H. Fuller (4th) enlarged ed., London and New York 1971, 361 (letter of 16.7.44).
4. S. Wiesenthal, *The Sunflower*, London 1970, 30ff.

III *The Anxiety of Christ*

1. S. Kierkegaard, *The Concept of Dread*, ET Princeton and Oxford 1944, 139 (translation altered).
2. E. Bloch, *Das Prinzip Hoffnung* I, Frankfurt 1959, 1 (ET *The Principle of Hope*, Oxford 1986). Passage translated direct from the German.
3. But this familiar translation does not bring out the particular force of the German. What Paul Gerhardt actually writes is: 'Then wrest me from my *fears* through thy *fear* and suffering' ('Dann reiss mich aus den Ängsten/kraft deiner Angst und Pein').
4. See ch. II, note 3 above.
5.   Ich hang und bleib auch hangen
            an Christus als ein Glied.
            Wo mein Haupt durch ist gangen,
            da nimmt es mich auch mit.
            Er reisset durch den Tod,

durch Welt, durch Sünd, durch Not,
er reisset durch die Höll,
ich bin stets sein Gesell.
6. C. Wesley, 'And can it be . . .'
7. But again (cf. n. 3) the German counterpart to Isaac Watts' hymn stresses the significance for the believer of Christ's *fear*.
Für dein Angst und tiefe Pein
will ich ewig dankbar sein.

V *The Resurrection of Christ – Hope for the World*

1. D. F. Strauss, *Die christliche Glaubenslehre* I, Tübingen and Stuttgart 1840, 71.
2. E. Troeltsch, 'Über historische und dogmatische Methode in der Theologie' (1898) in *Gesammelte Schriften* II, Tübingen 1913, 729–753 (ET 'Historical and Dogmatic Method in Theology' in *Religion in History*, trans. J. L. Adams and W. F. Bense, Edinburgh 1991).

VI *The Cosmic Christ*

1. Printed in F. Lüpsen (ed.) *Neu Delhi Dokumente* . . ., Witten 1962, 300–311. Sittler was expanding ideas already put forward by A. D. Galloway in *The Cosmic Christ*, London 1951.
2. W. Heisenberg, *Der Teil und das Ganze*, Munich 1969, 324f. (ET *Physics and Beyond*, trans. A. J. Pomerans, London and New York 1971.)
3. J. von Eichendorff, trans. F. Herzog.
4. Teilhard de Chardin, 'Christ the Evolver' in *Christianity and Evolution*, trans. R. Hague, London 1971, 147.
5. *Letters from a Traveller* (8 Sept. 1955), London 1967, 161.
6. *The Future of Man*, trans. N. Denny, London and New York 1964, 268 (translation altered).
7. *Christianity and Evolution*, 155f.
8. *The Future of Man*, 147.
9. Ibid. 152.
10. W. Benjamin, 'Theologisch-politisches Fragment' in *Illuminationen. Ausgewählte Schriften*, Frankfurt 1961, 280f. (Not included in ET published 1970, reprinted 1973, 1992.)
11. Ibid.

VII *Jesus between Jews and Christians*

1. M. Buber, *Der Jude und sein Judentum*, Cologne 1963, 41.

2. G. Scholem, 'Zum Verständnis der messianischen Idee', *Judaica* I, Frankfurt 1963, 73.

3. M. Buber, *Werke* II, Munich 1964, 388.

4. G. Scholem, 'Verständnis', 20.

5. G. von Rad, *Old Testament Theology* II, trans. D. M. G. Stalker, Edinburgh and London 1965.

6. M. Buber, *Werke* III, 756.

7. W. Benjamin, *Illuminationen. Ausgewählte Schriften*, Frankfurt 1961, 279. (See ch. VI n. 10.)

8. G. Scholem, 'Verständnis', 34.

9. Ibid. 73f.

10. F. Rosenzweig, *Der Stern der Erlösung*, 3rd ed., Heidelberg 1954, III, 67 (ET *The Star of Redemption*, London 1971). The phrase here is translated directly from the German.

11. Berakoth 57b.

12. M. Buber, *Der Jude und sein Judentum*, 562.

13. Schalom Ben-Chorin, *Die Antwort des Jona. Zum Gestaltwandel Israels*, Hamburg 1956, 99.

14. F.-W. Marquardt, 'Feinde um unsretwillen' in his *Verwegenheiten*, Munich 1982, 311.

VIII *'Behold I Make All Things New'*: The Great Invitation

1. C. Blumhardt, *Ansprachen, Predigten, Reden, Briefe 1865–1917* II, ed. J. Harder, Neukirchen 1978, 131.

2. M. Luther, *Von der Bereitung zum Sterben* (1519).

3. H. Schlier, *Wort Gottes. Eine neutestamentliche Besinnung*, 2nd ed., Würzburg 1962.

Index of Names

Machovec, M., 72
Maimonides, 112
Marquardt, F.-W., ch. VII n. 14
Moltmann, J., 2ff., 26, 30f., 48,
   58f., 69f., 143f.
Moreno, J. R., 48f.

Nietzsche, F., 100

Plato, 86

Rad, G. von, 111, 113, ch. VII n. 5
Rahner, K., 106
Romero, O. A., 39, ch. II n. 2
Rosenzweig, F., ch. VII n. 10

Schlier, H., 145, ch. VIII n. 3
Schmidt, K.-L., 120
Scholem, G., 111, 112, 116f.,
   ch. VII nn. 2, 4, 8 and 9

Schweitzer, A., 102
Sittler, J., 90, ch. VI n. 1
Sobrino, J., 40, 49, ch. II n. 2
Socrates, 72
Spartacus, 39, 62
Strauss, D. F., 76, ch. V n. 1

Teilhard de Chardin, P., 94, 99f.,
   104, ch. VI nn. 4–9
Tertullian, 60
Troeltsch, E., 77f., ch. V n. 2

Vogel, H., 55

Watts, I., ch. III n. 7
Werner, G., 22
Wesley, C., ch. III n. 6
Wichern, J. H., 22
Wiesel, E., ch. II n. 1
Wiesenthal, S., 40, ch. II n. 4

152